COUNTRY BOY GONE SOLDIERING

George H. Waple,
Soldier Retired

Combat Infantry Badge

ISBN: 978-1-60388-076-3
1-60388-076-3

Fourth Printing

COUNTRY BOY
GONE SOLDIERING

George Henry Applewhite
Captain, Army Enlisted
States, Retired
Caroline — Infantryman

Best Wishes

Marilyn Monroe and 1st Lieutenant Waple, Korea 1954

I have a tough assignment for you George, meet Marilyn Monroe at the helicopter pad at 3 a.m. As she walked down the exit stairway her face was pink from the cold, yet beautiful. She was followed by another great-looking lady, Mrs. "Lefty" O'Doul. My heart throbbed. This was just one of the great assignments I undertook during my career in the Army. Meeting people like Colonels Patton and Wainwright, the Russians at the Elbe after landing on Normandy Beach and the march across Europe. Followed by such folks as President Truman, General Bradley, General Eisenhower, Mr. Averial Harriman, Mr. Marx, the toy tycoon, and many other distinguished individuals, including Joe DiMaggio.

I have learned over the years to speak the truth quietly and clearly, and listen to others; even the dull and apparently ignorant have a story, as do I. I have enjoyed my achievements, and have had a hell of a life coming from such modest means as you will read.

Dedicated to those 3rd Cavalry Troopers who served as cadremen in the training, leadership and example for the men of the 331st Regiment.

George H. Waple
First Sergeant
Regt Hq Co

16 21

ERECTED BY JOHN
WAPLE MARCHANT

This work is dedicated to the memory of "Mama" Nancy Clark Waple, 1880–1956, and "Papa" George Henry Waple II, 1876–1942. They instilled in me and my three brothers and four sisters the need to be accountable and "pay one's way." As I made decisions in life, I always considered if Mama and Papa would be proud of me.

My prayers for those who died to save my life and freedom and for those who walked, fought, and shed blood with me shall always be my friend.

CONTENTS

Once I heard two friends talking. One said, "You know, George does not have a college education." His friend answered, "If George had a college education, he would not be George Waple."

"You are the best Sergeant I've ever served under — your men will do anything for you."

PREFACE

At the suggestion of many relatives and friends, after hearing so many stories told by me of my family, my boyhood, military life, W.W.II., Korea, and post W.W.II period, to write a book, I agreed that my story should be told. I hope the readers will find it as interesting as I have in hearing of my ancestors and living my life.

Special thanks to Robert Gibson Corder, born in Culpepper, Virginia, and now living in Richmond, Virginia, who complied a genealogical history of the Waple Families of America.

This book is a collection of stories that I've read, been told of, and lived. A collection of facts, legends, reminiscences, and tales as I've lived them. I never really had a way with words, so the story is told the way it was.

It is a story of a farm boy who was the youngest of eight, four girls and four boys. We were all born in the community of what is now called Waples Mill, Virginia. This mill was built by my great grandfather in 1867 on Difficult Run, the stream that would provide the water for the grist mill.

A story of a young boy, born of a humble background, who thought during those early years that this was the way it was. Never gave consideration to the fact that life was better some other place. Was never unhappy with life style because that is all that I knew, my daily routine was the way it was. Never dreamed of the day that I would leave home at the tender age of seventeen.

I was born there in 1921, lived there until 1938, when at the age of seventeen I joined the US Third Horse Cavalry at Fort

Myer, Virginia. Later I went into the Infantry and into Normandy in June 1944. Fought with the 331st Infantry of the Eighty Third Infantry Division from Omaha Beach to the Elbe River in Germany, where we met the Russians. Returned to Fort Myer in November 1945. Served there until 1952 when General Bradley, Chairman of the Joints Chief of Staff, commissioned me a Second Lieutenant. I fought with the 31st Infantry of the 7th Infantry Division in Korea for one campaign. which included participation in the War's last battle, taking place from "Ol' Baldy" across Chorwan Valley on July 26 and 27th.

I then became the aide to the Commanding General of the 7th Infantry Division. Served in the Canal Zone as aide to the US Army Commander, and later at Fort Leavenworth, Kansas, retiring from the Army 1 June 1962. From then until now I've been the best citizen that I know how to be.

* * *

During the summer of 1939, Colonel Patton led the 3rd Cavalry and the 16th field Artillery to the Battlefields of Manassas. As the battle began, my troop met Colonel Patton coming in the other direction.

Sir, Captain Dewey, Headquarters Troop reporting. "Get your troop the hell off the road and let these fighting soldiers pass," was the reply from Colonel George S. Patton who was leading "E" and "F" troops into battle – a sham battle at Manassas, Virginia during the summer of 1939. My duties in Headquarters Troop as a PVT Specialist 5th Class was radio operator of a horse mounted, hand cranked SRC-103-A radio with Morse code transmitting key strapped to my knee.

The Captain ordered Headquarters troops up on embankment and into a wooded area; I was mounted on a horse and was leading a packhorse with the radio mounted.

2

When we reached the crest of the bank, my horse stepped into yellow jacket nest. The bees swarmed out at my two horses, which began to jump. As I held the reins of my horse and held the lead reins of the radio packhorse, all hell broke loose; the radio packhorse finally broke loose and galloped away hitting tress with the SCR-103-A radio. Finally the girth straps broke and the radio went flying. When the dust settled and everything was under control, we continued our mission.

When we finally returned back to Fort Myer, I was charged with negligence of duty for letting the packhorse loose but finally beat the rap when they dropped the charges.

Country Boy Gone Soldiering is a record of a young man's journey from obscurity in a poor Virginia farm community founded by his great grandfather, to a productive interesting life where he made significant contributions fighting America's Wars, honoring its heroes, and supporting key leadership personalities and missions for the United States of America

COUNTRY BOY
GONE SOLDIERING

The George Henry Waple Family

"Momma" (1879-1956)

"Papa" (1879-1942)

**Left to right: Raymond, Rufus, Florence and George (standing);
Hazel, Lucy, Ralph and Francis (seated)**

6

Momma

Rufus Clark

Raymond Randolph

Ralph Eugene

Lucy Estelle

Hazel Pauline

Frances Isabelle

Florence Lorraine

George Henry

John Henry Waple   George Henry Waple   Hezekiah S. Waple
Grandfather   Great Grandfather
(1852-1924)   (1814-1904)   (Born 1854)

BEGINNING

It is Christmas Eve 1996, and I am 75 years old. It has been a warm windy day; I've walked on the golf course, hit some balls with my driver, and got exercise.

I've told about thousands of events during my adulthood, about all my walks of life, some sad, some funny, but mostly about the life of a country boy born at Waples Mill, Fairfax County, Virginia. People say, "George, you should write a book", so here it goes.

The Waple immigration to America evidently began in the late 1600's to early 1700's. It appears that Maryland was the first state in which these immigrants lived. In a genealogical history report, completed by a cousin of mine, reflects a shield in a coat of armor that was erected by a John Waple, merchant in Athlone, Ireland in 1621.

I wish to begin with a few words about my ancestors. My great grandfather was born on December 11, 1816, and lived in Piscataway, Prince George County, Maryland, but it has been also reported that he lived in Charles County. He moved some time between 1840 and 1843 to Philadelphia in the company of his first wife, Mary, and their first daughter Catherine Ann, and then on to Boggs Township in Clearfield County, Pennsylvania. After moving, two more daughters were born to Henry and Mary. In 1850 Henry Waple's occupation was listed as an Inn Keeper. The place of business was known as the Half Way House Tavern. He also was listed as a farmer in the 1860 census.

His first wife (Mary) died Dec 3, 1850, and he remarried March 16, 1851 to a girl named Sarah A. Litz, age 19, in Clearfield County. Sarah bore great grandpa two sons, one being my grandfather, John Henry. Sarah died May 22, 1855.

Great grandpa moved with his two sons, John and Hezekiah from Pennsylvania to Virginia in 1861. His political beliefs (he was a Democrat) were aligned with the South on the slavery issue, and therefore, found it impossible to continue to live in a hostile environment. Records reflect that he purchased a log home of two rooms and 137 acres farm in Fairfax County from a Mr. Andrew Cross on 11 May 1861 for $3,000.00. The log house, built some time early in the Eighteenth Century, with an addition added on later, still stands and remained with the Waple descendants until 1957. At this time it was sold along with fourteen acres to a Mr.

Reeder of Alexandria, Virginia who maintains it in its present state. It is a beautiful home and can be seen any time one is in the area. Mr. Reeder now calls the residence "Squirrel Hill."

Frances Thorpe Waple, wife of Henry Waple, my Great Grandfather, is buried in Vale Cemetery beside her husband.

George Henry Waple, better known as "Henry", married again to a Frances Thorpe, who was of Cherokee descent, April 28, 1864. Henry and his two sons, John and Hezekhiah farmed, and on October 16, 1866, bought property from the Gabriel Fox Estate on Difficult Run for the sole purpose of rebuilding a Water Grist Mill that was destroyed during the Civil War and previously owned by the Fox family, and to operate a saw mill on the same site. The mill went into operation in 1867. "Henry" operated the mill up to some time in the 1870's, when he turned the operation over to his oldest son, John Henry Waple, who became my Grandpa. John operated the Mill until 1903, when he sold it to a Mr. Edward Millard who operated the mill until 1913. Mr. Millard then sold the mill, a house across the road, and 30 acres, more or less, for $2,300 cash in hand back to my father, George Henry Waple II, who ran the mill until 1920, at which time it was torn down.

This undated photograph shows the Waple family's grist mill west of Fairfax City. Photo courtesy of the Fairfax County Public Library Photographic Archive.

The home my Great Grandfather purchased from Mr. Andrew J. Cross located in Northern Virginia, consisting of the house, 137 acres of land for $3,000 in May 1861.

Water for the mill operation was provided by damming Difficult Run, and diverting water down a mill race. Portions of which are still visible to this date.

The third child of John Henry Waple was, George Henry Waple II, named after his grandfather, and was born September 13, 1879. As a boy, he helped on the farm and with the mill operation. He also got a job at the Willard Farm in Fairfax Court House area. Willard, being of the family that owned the Willard Hotel in Washington D.C. His reported salary was $1.00 per day. On this salary, he got married, bought a home, and started a family.

George Henry Waple II, married Nannie B. Clarke, (born in 1880 and died in 1956) on Dec 4, 1901 in Vale Church, Vale, Virginia, on Fox Mill and Vale Roads. They first lived in a small house about 3/4 of mile northwest of Waples Mill on what is now Waples Mill Road.

My mother, Nannie Bessie Clarke, was born in King George County, Virginia. Her family moved up to the community of Vale, Fairfax County in the late eighteen nineties. Mama was a pretty girl and was a lay school teacher. She was also a religious Methodist lady and went to church at Vale Church, where she married my father. After marriage she moved to the Waples Mill Community and went to church in a small Methodist church at Waples Mill.

The first son died at birth and is buried at Vale Cemetery in the Waple plot beside his mom and dad. In this small two bed room house George and Nannie had five children, and in 1913 they bought the Mill and Saw Mill back from Mr. Millard as reflected previously. My papa, George H. Waple II, operated the mill and saw mill, plus farming the 30 or so acres until 1920 at which time he tore the mill down and built a small general store at the Junction of Fox Mill and Waple Mill Roads. Papa ran the store, farmed, bought more property, started buying and selling produce, i.e. chicken, eggs, calf or what ever the local farmers had to sell and would take them into Washington DC for resale. This was about an eighteen mile trip, and by horse and wagon it took about five hours to get there. He then bought more land, farmed, and huckstered buying and selling produce.

My father was never called up for W.W.I, he being a former mill operator and with five children by 1917, he just kept on doing his thing, farming and huckstering.

A Country Boy

MY BIRTH 1921

It was during the cold month of February that Mama would bring me into this world. Our living room was the only room with heat, and with me coming along at any time, Mama was put to bed downstairs on February sixth. I guess papa decided she should be warm. On the evening of February seventh Doctor Jones was sent for, and on the morning of February 8th I was born. They named me George Henry III, after Papa and my great Grandfather. Papa and Mama were 42 years of age at this time. The next morning as the story goes, my grandfather walked by and Papa yelled out, Nannie had a boy, going to call him George Henry. My Grandfather, getting old at this time, thought Papa said Nannie had twins going to name one George and the other Henry. My grandfather spread the news around the community.

At this time there was still a house full and I received a lot of attention. I slept with Papa and Mama until I was three or four. Then shifted in bed with my two sisters in the same room. I am sure things were rough in those days, as well as after, when the Depression came. The longest memory I have was at about the age of three or four when I got a tricycle for Christmas. I had gone to bed early the night Santa came, but was awakened at about 7 p.m. Christmas Eve being told that Santa had been there. I jumped on my tricycle and rammed directly into the tree, a six foot tall cedar. I broke a lot of the balls and made a mess. I was sent back to bed, but probably did not sleep very good that night as I was looking forward to Christmas morning and my bike. In those days we had no fancy pine trees that we have today, just scrawny old cedar. However, when trimmed, they looked pretty good. I can remember the corner of the parlor where it was placed, just to the left of the window that faced Fox Mill Road.

I have asked my older siblings often where we all slept. When I was a baby we only had two bedrooms. In my father's and mother's room there were two beds, one for them and one for Lucy and Frances. The room was small so it had to be cozy. My sister Lucy told me that after she got old enough to realize what my father and mother were doing at night she left the room and went into the next room to sleep with my two older sisters Hazel and Florence. I believe that my older brothers slept in the old general store house as there was a wood stove there for heat.

We did not have any inside facilities so we had to go to the outhouse if we had to go to the potty. It was terrible in the cold snowy weather. We had no toilet paper and would use the Sears and Roebuck or Montgomery Ward catalogs. After the soft tissues were used up it was rough. We had a two holer; I really don't know why because no two people would ever want to go at the same time. Papa never went there at all, he would go in the barn behind the horses and used a corn cob. When I got of age to where I would have to clean the stable, manure from behind the horses and cows. I hated to see his droppings there. I would cover them with horse dung and then shovel them out to the pile. By spring of every year that pile would be big. Papa or my older brother would haul it out to the grain fields for fertilizer.

My mother always had a "Pot" to use at night if someone had to go, especially on cold snowy nights. Mama would usually slide the pot under her bed if it would fit. Otherwise the receptacle would set on a piece of linoleum by the bed. The reason for the linoleum was that if someone missed the pot, it would not go into the floor and smell. This procedure was a mess to say the least. My mother would empty the "slop jar", as it was called, every morning. If there was only urine in it, she would throw it out the back yard. When there was snow on the ground it would create a yellowish stain in the snow. The older boys would not use this procedure, they would just raise the window and urinate. The tin porch roof had a yellow rust area all the way down to the edge.

Church as it looks today. My wife Violet stands in pulpit with two rose trees she made. The communion table was given to the Church by my Mama in the early fifties, God bless her soul.

I can remember going to this church as a young boy, I would use my cap to take up collection which was only nickels and dimes. One time a nickel slid in a hole of the lining of my cap and when I put the cap on, upon leaving the church I felt the nickel. I don't know what went through my mind maybe I meant to steal it for chewing gum, I don't know, but I did keep it. That moment has been with my conscious for at least seventy years. One of Papa's sisters, who was blind, played organ and her husband who had lost one arm in a railroad accident was the preacher. I don't think that he was ever ordained, but delivered the word to the best of his ability. There may have been five or six people in the congregation. Mama, sisters Frances, Lucy, and me made four. This church was torn down soon so we all went to church at Vale, a mile and a half away. In the winter, if the weather was real bad, we would not go. The church had two pot-bellied stoves that Uncle Jack, mama's brother, would start a fire early to heat up the building. He only lived several hundred yards up the road.

In the summer we would hold ice cream festivals behind the church under the two big trees. Sometimes there would be twenty or so people there plus a bunch of kids. We would play games and have loads of fun.

This church had its hundredth centennial several years ago. I attended and was asked to say a few words. I told some nice stories and some sad. I tried to be funny at times and had the congregation rolling in the isles. It was the first time that I had ever seen the church full. I told of Uncle Jack's wife who played the organ in those days. As she played while we sang, "When the roll is called up yonder" she would hit a sour note, with this, as young kids, we would laugh. This really provoked her. At least once each summer the congregation would go on a trip to Glen Echo, an amusement park on the North Bank of the Potomac River, up the river from Washington. Uncle Jack, Mama's brother, and some one else who owned a truck, would place straw in the bed of the truck and off we would go from the church yard. In those days, it would take about an hour to get there. Picnic lunches were made by all, and we stayed all day. What a time we would have riding the Ferris wheel, merry-go-round, and especially the electric bumper carts; the ones where one would push the accelerator pedal and steer, ramming into each other. This was so much fun. Everyone dressed in their "Sunday Best" to go to a meeting." I remember my stove pipe shorts.

The church records reflect that my grandfather devoted twenty hours of labor to the building of the church in the 1880's. In the cemetery behind the church I have my great grandfather, my mother, father, two brothers, and two sisters buried. Yearly I donate to the church for the sole purpose of the upkeep of the cemetery.

The two-room schoolhouse is just across the road where I attended the first grade and learned to draw.

In the main house there was a hole in the ceiling of the living room were a big pot-bellied stove was. My father would fill this stove at night with wood, close it up so the wood would not burn too fast. This stove created enough heat to allow some heat to go up through the hole for heat upstairs. This stove was in the living room, a room maybe, eight by ten. In addition to the stove, there was a cot, several chairs, and a battery operated radio.

Pop would listen to Amos and Andy, bank the stove with hickory wood, and go to bed. As we only had coal oil lamps (kerosene) there was not much light. As I went to school and had homework, it was hard to read and write to this light. As stated at first the house had two bedrooms, a living room and parlor. Off the back side was a lean-to porch where we stacked the wood and there was a small summer kitchen. It had a very low ceiling and was hot as hell in the summer time. This room had only a dirt floor. There was also a room off the back of the house that we used during the winter. Mama used a kerosene stove which had four burners. In the summer kitchen we had a wood stove at one time, but later

19

switched the kerosene stove there also. In the late twenties papa and old man Arman Trout built two more rooms onto the house.

Home purchased by George Henry Waple II from Ed Millard around 1913, the same time he re-bought the mill that was originally built by George Henry Waple I in 1866–67. This house is where I was born and raised. The left end was added around 1930. Prior to that there were only two bedrooms. At one time, there were eight children plus Papa and Mama residing there.

This section was as large as the old part and had only two rooms. It was a great improvement as we now had three bedrooms. In addition, our kitchen was big. The size of the room was about fifteen by thirty. Prior to our supper everyone but Papa would take a dish towel and gather at one end of the room, they then would walk across the room to shoo the flies forward to the screen door that I would hold open. There would be a swarm of them as with all of the traffic coming in and out during the day allowing them to enter. This was a daily chore before each supper meal. Mama would also hang those ugly sticky fly catchers from the ceiling of the kitchen and porches.

When I was a little boy I wore a buster brown haircut. When I started to get a regular hair cut, I was taken or rode a horse to Mr. Joe Crosin's general store at Pender. In addition to running the store he cut hair. I would sit on an orange crate. He had scissors and hand clippers. He also coughed a lot and would spit in a tin can nearby. If a customer came in to buy a loaf of bread or can of beans he would stop cutting and take care of the customer. He would often pass the time of day so there I sat waiting.

When I was about five or six, I guess Papa was repairing the roof and was using a ladder which was leaning against the house, my sister Fran and I were playing nearby in an old stuffed chair, the chair tilted over and I fell against the ladder which had a nail sticking out where a rung was placed. My head fell against the nail, just between my eyes an inch or so either way it would have gone into one of my eyes. Blood was wiped and a Band-Aid was applied. I don't know how long the Band-Aid was there, but one day my sister Florence, who had studied nursing, prior to becoming a telephone operator, came home from New York, took one look at my Band-Aid and immediately removed it. The hole from the nail was infected and maggots were in it. I guess it was a good thing she came home. Florence cleaned my sore, nursed it, and in time it healed. I still have the scar there.

Around the age of five or six, I started elementary school at Vale, which was about one and one half miles down the

21

road from home, with my sisters Lucy and Frances. The school had two rooms, a pot-belly stove, and an "out house." There probably was only ten or fifteen students ranging from the first grade (only me) to seventh. A cousin of mine, along with my sister Hazel, were teachers. Hazel taught there for a few years and then got married. My cousin, Miss Clarke, would assign lessons to each grade, two or three maybe in each grade, so by the time she go to me, she would tell me to color a mule and wagon. This happened every day. At the end of the year, the only thing I knew how to do was draw. I almost had a degree in drawing. I sure could draw a beautiful wagon with two mules pulling it.

The school board closed the school after my first year, so the entire community started at Oakton, a three and 1/2 mile walk. No buses in those days. When I reported to Mrs. Butts, God bless her cotton-pickin' soul, she taught the first grade for years and years. Mrs. Butts tested my ability, I couldn't read, write or nothing. She said, "What did you do at Vale School?" I said, "I drew pictures of two mules and a wagon, wanna see one?" She then stated, "George, if you had two white pigs and two black pigs in a pen, how many pigs would you have?" I answered, "a pen full of pigs." I repeated the first grade. At Vale however, we did have a lot of fun. The older boys would pretend that they were foxes and had the younger ones chase them. The foxes would climb a tree and we would bark at them like hound dogs, and if we didn't watch out, they would "pee" on us. I stayed in Oakton School for three years, first, second, and third grades.

Drawing of Vale School, as it looked around 1888.

I wish to say something about that three-and-a-half mile walk to Oakton School. In the winter with the snow and drifts, it was a rough trek. One time we were late because of the deep snow, and because we were late, we were kept after

Sisters Florence and Frances at 100th Centennial of School

school for punishment. Another time we were taking a short cut through the woods and I got tired of carrying my lunch, usually a mustard jar of milk, peanut butter and jam sandwich, and maybe a graham cracker. I asked my sister Fran to carry my lunch for me, and when she refused, I took my mustard jar full of milk and threw it at her, hitting her in the forehead making a small gash which bled a little. One other time we walked to school in knee-deep snow only to find the school was closed. So we struggled back home. Remember, there were no telephones or radio to announce school closings.

Dad **Mama**

My sister Lucy had a boyfriend at Oakton who came from a rich family, he would give me a nickel to buy candy to make points with Lucy. As I got older I helped with chores.

I would help my sister get in wood from the wood shed by wheelbarrow, or in the little red wagon I had gotten. In fact, I was nine years old before I realized that my first name wasn't "get wood."

Papa drank at times and was very mean when under the influence. I remember when one of my older brothers had not come home from the night before; he walked in at supper time the following day, the whole family was at the supper table when brother Rufus walked to the door of the kitchen, Papa being angry at him for not coming home the night before and helping with the chores of the day, and said a few words to my brother. Rufus answered back in a sassy tone and Papa picked up his water glass and threw it at Rufus hitting him in the head. Rufus left, never to return home on a permanent basis again.

After the kitchen glass throwing incident between my father and Rufus, Rufus left and landed a job as a manager of a farm in Connecticut. One day on the job he was mixing lime to make white wash for fence painting, and the lime substance exploded burning his face, hands, and arms. After he recovered he returned to Fairfax. This is when he bought me a saddle and bridle for my pony. Rufus was never one for hard work so he began to find other means of support. He met a lovely widow who had one son and they married. This lady was originally from Leesburg, Virginia, and one from a family of fourteen, eleven girls and three boys. Ten of these girls were beautiful, but one was the black sheep, she was nice, but not so attractive.

Rufus liked to gamble, soon learned book making and set up shop in Falls Church, Virginia, in a small general store used as a front. Later he moved his office to the basement of his new wife's home just up the street. From there he moved to the garage in the rear of the house converting the garage

26

into a plush office. He had several men working for him now. He kept moving up, relocating often. Later he had the reputation of being one of the two bookies in the Washington DC area. His only competition was an old family who manufactured barrels in the Georgetown section. Wasn't too long before he owned race horses, and had his own plane to fly from track to track. At times he was loaded, and treated me good. He could flip out a twenty dollar bill anytime. He bought and operated a night club on Route 301 in Maryland for a while. It had a bar, restaurant, dance hall, and slot machines. As he referred to the girls, he had a bunch of "chippies" there too. Let the good times roll was his motto.

His lovely wife was a jewel, she moved from her house to a bigger home, then moved again. This all lasted until the early fifties when Congress cracked down on his business. He got into trouble with the IRS and others. When the good times ended he went into real estate, but had to operate under the table with a broker. I heard that he pulled off some great deals, in fact, he bought one of the farms where Dulles Airport is now located.

Even after the good times ended, he still put on a big front. Later as they lived in a condo, his wife taking a job in a department store at Seven Corners, Falls Church, the two of them always looked good. Rufus had made many friends, had paid off a lot of people, and could always find an open door. It was always a pleasure when I visited him and his wife, Virginia. It was a sad day when I helped to lay him to rest. He went from "Dog Patch" at Waples Mill to the top, only to fall. May he rest in peace.

Another time my sister Frances talked back to Papa and he beat her with a stick of stove wood. After her graduation from Oakton High that year she too left home to become a beautician. Brother Ralph left early as did sister Florence.

27

Flo went to New York City with a friend and became a telephone operator. She married a New Yorker and stayed there until the late 1940's when she and her husband returned home and bought a small house on Waples Mill Road. Papa only whipped me twice as I recall, the first time was when I was about four years old. The whole family had typhoid fever and Dr. Jones had come to give us shots. I had a baby pet duck that was running loose on the porch floor and Doctor Jones stepped back only to squash my duck. I had learned to talk and knew a few choice bad words which I used. Papa took a piece of egg crate board and spanked my butt real good. The other time was when I was about ten, he told me to go to the barn and get a piece of harness for him, I didn't react quick enough so he went himself. Upon returning to the team of horses he had to pass me. In doing so he grabbed me by the arm and beat me from my neck to my knees with this piece of rope. I never forgot that whooping. Because of Papa's actions at times, the shortage of living space, and conditions, is why, in my opinion, my older sister and brothers left home at an early age. However, I do wish to point out, we may have been as poor as church mice, but we never went to bed hungry. To top off the pudding, I want to say that we had the best mother ever to come along. She was a handsome lady, a great Ma, and cook. She made everything from scratch, great cakes, pies, griddle cakes, and biscuits.

I was her baby boy from the time I was born until she died in 1956. After I left home at age of seventeen to join the Army in 1938, I never missed going to see her or call her at least once a week. During W.W.II, I rarely missed sending her a note to state that I was OK, and that I loved her.

While in Europe, I received a picture of her with a notation on the back of it saying that every morning at nine o'clock she would say a prayer for me. I carry that picture to this day in my wallet and proudly show it to all my friends. I usually cry when I do so. I sure loved that lady. She took a lot of abuse, survived the worst of times, had nine babies with miscarriages as they came along, but still remained strong. I don't believe there was birth control in those days, but if there was, Papa and Mama never used any.

When mama and my sisters would have their monthlies, they would use old torn sheets, wash them and hang them on the clothes line. All of the boys knew what they were, and with four sisters and Mama, sheets were hanging almost all of the time. My sister Lucy told me a story that one time our father was drinking and was threatening Mama, so our mother took Lucy and Frances and ran to the creek and hid under some over hanging brush. As they sat in the water there was a reddish tint to the water where our mother sat. Lucy at first thought Mama was hurt, but she wasn't, it was nature taking place.

Being raised as we were, seeing animals breed, cattle, horses, pigs, dogs and poultry, I learned about sex at an early age. My older brother and the neighboring boys would always talk about it. They would draw pictures of girl's privates on the barn doors and other places, like the outhouse. As I look back, it was like tobacco road or worse.

I never mentioned my older sister Hazel, she was the apple of Papa's eye. She graduated from high school and went to a teachers college to become a school teacher. She did not teach long as she got married and started her own family. She was the sweetest sister one could ask for. Always loved me to her dying day. Actually, being the baby of the family, all my sisters and brothers were good to me.

I remember as a young boy there was always activity around the place. We had the animals and poultry to care for and to eat. We raised pigs for food. Papa would slaughter a steer for winter food. Papa functioned as the community veterinarian. He could castrate pigs, baby bulls to become a steer, and alter horses to become gelding. I've seen him deliver calves and baby horses; he did a whole lot.

There is nothing on a pig that one cannot eat. At least we ate the entire pig, the brain, tongue, guts, called "Chittlings", feet, and grind the scrap for sausage. We had the ham and shoulders, and the sides for bacon. Pig was good eating. Mama canned most of the meat for winter.

For a supplement to our farm diet, in the spring before any garden crops came in, papa would go fishing in the Potomac River, just North of the Old Chain Bridge. He would stand on some rocks and dip a net attached to a ten or twelve foot pole and catch herring swimming up stream to spawn. Some times he would catch three or four burlap bags full. Once in a while mixed in with the herring would be a shad, a much better eating fish over the herring. The shad is a salt-water fish that would come up the Potomac to spawn. The roe of this fish would make a beautiful meal. Back home Papa would dump these herring into a barrel with brine. During the rest of the year we would eat these herring. They were full of bones and salty. It would take me five minutes or so just to eat one, slim pickens.

There was always "Bee Honey" available. During the summer, occasionally, a swarm of bees would fly over, one could hear them coming off in a short distance because of the "Hum" the swarm would make. Papa would tell all of us kids to run in the house and get a pot, pan, or what ever we could to make noise with. This would attract the bees to land locally, build a hive, and manufacture honey. One time the swarm landed at the sill of the end window of the house above the cellar door. They found a hole in the clap board siding and settled in. That winter Papa smoked the bees and took all of the honey that was stored there. However, it was not always so convenient. The bees would normally find a hollow tree to create their new hive. The next winter papa and my older brother would chop the tree down and nab the honey. It was sure good on Mama's biscuits.

My sisters Lucy and Fran worked in the garden and I was their helper. We weeded the vegetables, picked strawberries, black berries, or whatever else was ripe. When picking wild blackberries we would get "chiggers," a small red parasite that would get under you skin. It would itch like heck. To kill these rascals we would take the cork of the turpentine bottle and dab the spot with turpentine. One time in doing this some turpentine ran down my spine into the crack of my behind. When it got to my backside it started to burn real bad. It set me on fire. I was naked at the time, but I ran out of the screen door, made several circles of the yard and returned to the back porch. My mother had just set a pan of milk down that she was going to skim the cream off of for butter. I sat down in it to soothe my tail. I sure caught hell for this act.

Taking care of the farm was not easy. We had to pack the hay in the barn, and push it back, boy it was hot. Luckily the creek was close by so we would wash off later. Papa always had a big garden which looked great. It never had weeds because we pulled them by hand as there was no weed killers in those days. My father was tough, but a good provider, he worked from sun up to sun down. He use to say, "get most of the work done before the heat of the day." I remember when he would be using the team of horses that he came to the house about 10 or 11 o'clock, unhitched the horses, and let them graze in the yard. If old Pat, the gelding, would urinate, it would kill the grass if he were hot and sweaty.

One time my brother, Raymond, who turned out to be the best friend I ever had, took me sledding. Unfortunately, Mama had given me some castor the night before, and as we were going down the hill we hit a plowed fire burm, a space that had been plowed three or four furrows wide to prevent a forest fire from spreading. Well, I "pooped" in my pants. I had on long underwear, so he undressed me there in the snow, taking off my long johns and redressed me. We tied the long johns on the back of the sled leaving a brown trail in the snow all the way home.

While on the subject of my best buddy, brother Ray, I tagged along with him whenever I could. He became a great shot, he could bag at least two quail on every covey flushed. With a twenty two caliber rifle, he would have me throw a tin can into the air, and he could usually keep the can airborne with three shots, bang, bang, bang. When the can hit the ground there would be three holes in it.

Brother Raymond was nine years older than me. One time when we were walking to the swimming hole, I guess I was about eight, he told me that not only was he my brother, he was my buddy. I never forgot that statement. In later years he proved this to be more than true.

Wild fox grapes grew along the banks of the creek. I would wade in the water and pick them off in a bunch. Sometimes when under the overhanging vines, that were attached to the brush, a snake would sliver off. Not harmful, but a little scary. I would sell the grapes at the market along with my goldfish, water cress, and squabs. I too, was becoming a huckster.

When we would have a summer thunder storm the creek would rise and overflow. There was a bridge by our house and I would jump off the bridge into the swirling water, and swim down stream for several hundred yards. Sometimes there would be snakes swimming with me.

One hot summer day, as I was walking to the swimming hole, I heard a squeal of a rabbit nearby. I made my way up the bank of the cut in the road, advancing toward the squeal. Upon reaching a brush pile, I noticed the front end of a small rabbit sticking out of the mouth of a larger black snake. A black snake will catch a small rabbit and excrete saliva on its body and swallow it. I got there just in time. Knowing that a black snake is not dangerous, I grabbed the snake just behind its head and squeezed. With this, it opened its mouth, allowing the rabbit to go free. I held on to the snake, and with my other hand grabbed its body to get good control of the snake. I then slid my hand back a few inches from the snake's head, and then snapped its head on a tree limb killing it. All in growing up in the country, save a rabbit to shoot later, and kill a black snake to boot.

In the thirties, my father built a pond, I guess about a half acre or so. We stocked it with goldfish. I would catch the small ones in a net, put them in a quart mason jar and sell three for a quarter. Watercress also grew at the water's edge. I would cut it, put it in a small bunch, place a rubber band around it, and sell it for a nickel. We also skated on the pond in the winter and would build a bonfire along the shore to stay warm.

Papa and the older boys were still huckstering at this time and I'd go to the market in Washington DC at 5th and Florida Ave., where we had a stand. It was a long day. I recall in my early years that Papa was a tough and rough man. He expected a lot from his help, whether it be his boys or hired help. Yet, I believe he was generally fair. I soon learned however, as I got older, why my older sisters and brothers left home at an early age.

We had a large yard and when my turn came I had to mow it with a push mower, it would take all day. However, we did save on electric, gas, and oil, you just packed your guts out. In the summer, all of the neighborhood boys and girls would come to our house. We would play ball, hide and seek, high over, red dog, and croquet. Everyone would have lots of fun, and even Papa would join in at times.

My father had the only radio in the area. For electricity he used a twelve volt battery. The cone shaped speaker was set in the living room window so everyone could hear. During the prize fights Papa would have a crowd there. When the battery would loose its power, one of my brothers would take it over to Fairfax Court House and get it charged at the Chevrolet Dealership.

When my mother went to the center market in Washington, sometimes I would go. However, I usually was left home with my older sisters. Once after the market day was over, my mother stopped in Georgetown to purchase some items from the five and dime store. I tagged along holding on to my mother's long dress. Momentarily, I let loose of my mothers dress, and regrabbed another dress without looking up. I followed along for a while, and when I did look up realizing I had latched onto a black lady's dress, I sure did let out a scream. I thought I was lost, but soon found my mother. I am sure the nice black lady did not want any part of this ugly freckled-face boy.

Earlier, when I was a little boy still nursing, my mother had a nice colored lady come and help her some. This lady had a baby about my age who was also nursing. Sometimes I would nurse on her other breast when her baby was having lunch. Black or white, the milk tasted the same.

After the horse and wagon days, Papa bought an old Oakland truck that Rufus or Raymond drove to go through

34

the country with Papa to buy up produce, this was called huckstering. Papa used a graduated type spring pull down scale when buying poultry from the farmer up in the country. He would tie four or five chickens' legs together with cord and then hook the cord onto the scale hook. As the pound lever was pulled down over the face of the scale, it would reflect the number of pounds the poultry was weighing. If Papa held the scale in the palm of his hand and raise the scale head high, the correct weight would appear a pound or so lighter than it actually was. This procedure gave him an advantage of a pound or so to make up for losses as he stated, a clever act. Sometimes on the way home from the market Papa would buy a bushel of oysters at the fish market. He would sit in front of the wood stove oven and place several dozen of them in the oven. As they would open, because of the heat, he would snap them apart with an oyster knife, cut the attachment, and slurp them off the half shell. Once in a while he would hand me one, saying, "Here boy, eat this oyster, it will make you grow to become a big strong man. Papa would shuck what he didn't eat from the oven, and Mama would make oyster stew or fried oysters, boy, they were good.

I learned from my brothers about bounty hunting. In those days there was a bounty on hawks and crows. They would set a steel trap on a pole to catch the hawk, but would shoot the crow. We would get a quarter per head. Later on, as I got older, I would go into the pine forest, find a crows nest, climb the tree, shoot the old crows, and take the young. This was cruel, but profitable, .25 cents a head. I learned a lot from my older brothers Raymond, Rufus, and the neighborhood boys.

At about ten years of age, Papa bought me a pony, a black shetland, but it was a little wild as it had been running loose on a farm. My brother Rufus bought me a saddle and bridle. I rebroke the pony, and we had fun. Papa also bought me my first two-wheel bicycle, a used one that I painted red. I also remember the first time that I went rabbit hunting. Papa found a rabbit sitting in his nest and told me to just shoot its nose off, so as not to spoil the rest of the meat. I tried to be too tricky and missed his nose. The rabbit ran off and Papa gave me hell, another lesson learned. One time when I was about 12, Papa sent me down to a patch of woods where there was a lot of squirrels. It was a rainy September morning and I was in school. I took nine shells for his 20 gauge and I had a good shoot, bagged nine squirrels with nine shells. Papa gave me hell for not taking more shells. I was glad the school bus came. Mama would cook squirrel many different ways, baked, broiled, and fried. She would boil the older ones first. This was the same with the many rabbits we ate.

Another time I was rabbit hunting, I guess I was 13 or 14, it had to be a Saturday because I was home, I jumped a rabbit, shot and killed it. I was on another man's property who did not like the Waples. Monday morning the cops came to the school and arrested me for trespassing. I had to call my brother Rufus, as we did not have a phone at home, to come and bail me out. A few years later, the same man came out when Rufus and a few of his friends were fox hunting. The man yelled at my brother. With this, Rufus hit the man in the mouth with a flashlight. A few days later he got arrested. This mean man drove to work and passed my house at the same time every day. As he crossed the bridge over Difficult Run, his car tires would pick up a couple of nails that I had placed there. Soon he would have a flat tire, sweet revenge.

During my early youth, I became pretty good at marbles. I had a good batch of them that I carried in a bull durum bag.

Before school, at recess, and lunch break, I would run to the marble playing area and take on all comers. At home my older sisters or cousins would play with me outside the kitchen door. I would also use marbles to shoot at birds, tin cans, or any thing else with my sling shot. We use to call that a bean shooter, great fun.

For another enjoyment, I would push a small rim from a tricycle or maybe a larger rim from a carriage. To push the small rim, I would take about a three-foot stick and attach a cross bar at the bottom about eight inches long, I would push this wheel for hours, good exercise, but would run yourself silly going up and down the dirt road or around the yard. I've never seen that type of fun performed by any youngsters since those days. I would also take an old tire, go to the top of the orchard hill out back, get inside the tire and roll down the hill ramming into the hay stacks to stop, another great sport.

I had a fox terrier named Tiny when I was a boy, which I taught how to chase rabbits and squirrels. In the winter time we would go into the woods and chase a squirrel into a knot in a tree, she would bark and I would run to the tree. I then would cut a long thin limb from a bush or tree and stick the poke into the hole, twist it until the end became wrapped around the squirrel tail. When I could not twist any longer, I knew that I had it secure. I then would pull the squirrel out, killing it with another stick or object that I had in my other hand. My pup and I would then proceed for another catch, fried squirrel for supper.

If I came upon a thicket of berries and honeysuckle I would take a stone and roll it into the bushes telling my dog to "sickem," she would run into the thicket, and if there was a rabbit in there she would chase it out. I would shoot the rabbit with my 410 gauge shot gun. Maybe Mama would cook squirrel and rabbit for supper.

In my early years I would help gather chestnuts. This was before the national blight that killed these beautiful trees. In our area of the country, there were many trees still alive and produced a beautiful nut. The burr would fall to the ground, we would then trounce or hit the burr with a stick and the nut would fall out. I then could pick up a bag full of nuts. Those trees were also used for the rail fences throughout the South in the older times. The logs would be split and made into rails. The rails would be placed on top of each other in a zig-zag fashion to make the fence. These lines of rail fences over the farm land were beautiful. Only a few stand today.

Another nut bearing foliage in our area was a bush that grew about eight to ten feet tall. It developed into a bush with maybe twenty or so limbs grown from the ground. This bush also had burrs, and in late summer would open and a small nut about the size of one's finger nail would fall to the ground. To rush this procedure, my sisters and I would take an old sheet, place it on the ground, bend the foliage over and hit it with a long stick. We would then release these limbs, and on the sheets would be full of these burrs. We then would pick the sheet up at the corners, shake it allowing the burrs to be at the top. We then would throw the burrs away finding all of the little nuts to be at the bottom. I would fill some bull durum bags with these nuts and take them to school with me and eat them throughout the day. The meat of the nut was very tasteful. We called these nuts "chinkapins." To this day, I don't know where the name originated.

In the early twenties a confederate soldier bought the farm across the creek. There was a three-bedroom house and forty-five acres of land. His name was John Chin. Mr. Chin was blind at the time he moved in, but was helped around by his wife and children. After I was old enough to visit his house he would talk to me. He sat in a rocking chair fully dressed, black trousers, shirt, tie, and coat. He chewed tobacco and his family provided a can, size of a large coffee can, for him to spit in. Naturally, much of this missed the can, some on his trousers and shoes, some in the can. Mrs. Chin did not keep a very tidy house and my Mama did not like for me to go there as they coughed all the time. Mama said they all had consumption. I even ate there at times and my mother would scold me if she found out about it. Mr. and Mrs. Chin had three sons who worked for my father. As they got older, my father would send me over to their house to wake them up. I would go upstairs to their room to wake them and could hardly stand the smell. I realized this as a little boy and can still remember that odor. They never bathed and their sheets were dingy. How that has stuck with me.

At this writing, there are two of the Chin girls living. One of them, Minnie, still owns the farm. It is located at Waples Mill about sixteen miles from Washington DC. I visited her in the spring of 1996. Minnie doesn't tell her age, but she has to be in her nineties. She has lost some of her spark and thought I was my older brother, Ralph, whom she liked as a young girl. I asked her why she didn't sell the farm and her reply was, "I don't need the money." The place has got to be worth ten million. I have a picture of her and I, it is a beauty.

With Minnie, who died a millionaire, but didn't know it.

As stated before, all of my sisters and brothers left home at an early age. Frances, four years older than I, was a smart cookie. She graduated from Oakton High School at the age of sixteen. She was the star and captain of the basketball team, a real pretty girl. Frances got a job in a beauty parlor after graduation as she was a natural beautician. After W.W.II Frances was still working for the owners. On my arrival home I chipped in and helped her buy a recently vacated beauty shop down the street from where she worked. I had saved some money during the war and we borrowed the remainder that we needed from brother Rufus. The shop that Frances left soon closed as Frances took all of her customers to her new shop. We then bought that shop, and now had two. We soon paid Rufus off, and when I got my initial investment back, I gave my share to her. She remained in the business all of her life.

After all of the others left home, I was there alone with Papa and Mama. I had my own room, and now we were like uptown folks, we had a guest room.

My brother Raymond met a real nice girl from Clifton, Virginia, and it wasn't long before they got married. Our guest room was taken, and in February 1933, my sister-in-law had a baby boy. Doctor Myers and my Papa delivered the baby, a boy named Hugh. It was a cold winter night, the same as it had been when I was born.

As I grew older Papa bought more land and farmed. We had two horses, Pat and Beauty, that we used to plow and cultivate. We would hoe the corn and other crops. We had a great garden with mama canning almost everything. Mama canned pork sausage from pigs, and anything else that would keep in mason jars. She canned all vegetables, corn, etc. We stored canned food in a dirt cellar under the house.

We killed pigs for food, and had poultry of all kinds for food. We ate good, but did not realize how poor we were. Papa, I don't think had more than a hundred dollars at any one time. If he needed money he would go to the bank president, usually a friend, borrow what he needed and returned it with very little interest. My father would go through the country, later on, in the old truck, that one of my brothers drove, (Papa never learned to drive) and buy hundreds of turkeys for Thanksgiving and Christmas. They would roost on the out buildings and trees around the house. About four days before Thanksgiving, we would drive them into the barn and then tie about 10 or 12 on a stake rigged close by and cut their throats. We would then dip them into scalding water so that feathers could be removed easily. Papa would hire eight or ten people from the community to remove or pick the feathers from the body of the turkeys. We would then place them in the stream to cool them out. After being in the water for an hour or so we would hang them on the rafters of the cellar until we packed them into the trucks on straw. The next day they were taken to Washington, DC for sale. This went on for three or four days prior to Thanksgiving. That was quite an operation in those days. My father would make several hundred dollars from this operation. He would return the loan to the bank with a few dollars interest. One time after the turkeys where placed in the stream to cool out, Lucy and Frances were assigned the task of keeping turtles away from them. They forgot to pay close attention as they played in the water. The turtles came, as did our father, and he spanked those girls good for messing around after he had assigned them a chore.

We also always had a great garden, fruit from the orchard and meat from the farm. For the animals we raised oats and corn. One time Papa planted about eight acres of sweet corn. Upon harvest it was placed in burlap bags and sold for two cents per ear.

My older brothers would hunt wild game for food, such as rabbits and squirrels. I was taught at an early age to do the same. I would trap rabbits for resale and food. My older brothers would also set a trap line along the brook for mink, muskrats and the like. Papa had a large pack of hounds, mostly fox hounds, but he also had what we called night dog. He would hunt opossum, raccoons, and skunk, and would sell their furs in Washington DC. With his fox hounds Papa would hunt foxes catching them by shooting or running them into a den and digging them out. He would kill them and sell the pelts. One year we captured twenty-eight foxes, Papa was proud. As he would place the pelts on a stretching board and hang them at the end of the wood shed to dry.

My father had a great pack of hounds he could tell each by their bark. While they were on the chase, he'd say "listen, Lighting is leading the chase - no - now ol' Thunder has taken over." I believe they will cross the road at the "dip" of the dirt road in Hoags Woods, hurry boys, run up there and shoot the fox as he comes out of the woods." Ninety percent of the time he was right. One cute story he use to tell was about a friend of his from Washington, DC, who was a judge. He came out to our farm to go fox hunting with my father. As they sat on the knoll in a pasture land belonging to a neighbor, Papa stated, "Listen judge, ain't that beautiful music?" The judge replied, "I can't hear any music because of the damn dogs barking." Papa knew his hounds well and could tell the direction they were going. He could tell if it was a red or gray fox when it went up a leaning tree or in a den. He always walked, knowing where to go to hear the best chase.

If my father wanted to show off his dogs and have a visitor hear a good chase, he would place about twenty or so herring into a burlap bag and tie the bag to a long rope. I would saddle old Beauty and drop the bag of fish over a pre-arranged trail. His fox hounds would chase this scent as if it were a real fox. We could make this chase go as long as Papa wished, and over an area where the hounds could be heard. Papa's guests were usually impressed.

Through Northern Virginia fox hunting was a great sport, even among the poor folks. Papa had friends from his huckstering days from around Haymarket, Manassas, Gainesville, Marshall, and Leesburg, all of which, like my father, had a pack of fox hounds. If Papa could get anyone to drive him, off he would go to visit some of the ol' boys and go on a fox chase. One time my brother-in-law, Clark Jones, sister Hazel's hubby, drove him. On return that late Saturday afternoon, Clark parked in the gully in front of the house with Papa, drunk as a skunk on the back seat. Froth was rolling out of his mouth from the moon shine, with flies all over. It was an awful site for us kids to see. The next morning it was business as usually with Papa and Mama, as Lou, Fran, and I were off to Sunday School.

One time I was fox hunting with Papa and he developed a toothache. We walked through the woods about three miles to a dentist at Oakton. He walked in and told the dentist to pull the aching tooth. Without any pain killer, the dentist reached in and yanked the tooth out. We retraced our tracks and found the hounds running a fox.

In the late thirties a retired admiral bought a farm about three and a half miles down the road. After he had passed our home several times, Papa stopped him. The Naval graduate was asked who he was, where was he from, where he now lived, and so forth. The Admiral became fascinated with my father. He then would stop every time he drove by. They became great friends with the Admiral listening to the tales Papa would tell. Papa also introduced him to fox hunting.

He would walk with my father hours on end listening to Papa and the fox hounds chase the fox. He took pictures of Papa throughout the day, some of Papa just listening to the hounds or cupping his penis as he took a leak. All of this country living was new after being on a boat during his career.

During the late 20's to early 30's, Mama started raising turkeys. Papa had fenced about an eight-acre field with a fence about eight feet tall. She started by having hen turkeys lay eggs, and hatch them. Naturally, there had to be a gobbler or two present. A year or two later she started buying baby turkeys and raising them in a poultry house Papa had built. I believe she started with several hundred babies. As the turkeys got older we would move them to this large fenced in field. This was Mama's project. Papa farmed and hauled produce. I had to help Mama carry water and feed for these turkeys. We each carried an eight to ten quart bucket of water about 400 yards. In the late summer of July, August, and September, this was a chore as there had to be plenty of water. We would slaughter these turkeys at Thanksgiving and take them to Washington DC for retail at the old center market.

From the time that I was knee high to a grasshopper I would fish in the creek near our house. I would cut a pole and then tie a piece of cord to it, use a sinker cork and hook. Then I would go behind the barn where the soil was rich and dig for worms. The creek would have some spots where it was three or four feet deep, these areas were made of high water usually on a bend in the creek or under the tree roots where the soil had been washed away. I would catch a perch, sucker, or small catfish. After I had caught two or three, I would take them to Mama so proud of my catch. Mama would give me a sweet smile and would cook them for me in a frying pan on top of a wood cook stove. They were delicious. In the spring, when the fish were coming up stream to lay their eggs, I could catch some good size suckers by feeling under the bank and grab them with my hand. During the winter, when the creek was frozen, I would walk on the ice with an ax or sledge hammer. Upon seeing a fish under the ice, I would hit the ice over the fish and stun it, then I would chop a hole in the ice and fetch it out. Mama would be proud of my achievement and I would have more fried fish.

For bathing we had a wash tub. Mama would heat a bucket of water and mix it with cold water so we would have enough water in the tub to bath. Before Fran and Lucy left home, I was the third one to get washed.

My mother always kept a willow switch on top of the stoves warming closet. If I passed her or misbehaved in any fashion, she would cut my legs with that willow switch, it had a lasting effect. But, of course, it hurt her almost as it did me having to punish her baby.

One time when I was in high school I sprained my ankle playing some sport. I had to report to the school nurse to have it checked. As we only bathed infrequently, and I took my shoe and sock off I had grime behind my ankle. I wet my finger with my tongue and tried to rub it off before the nurse could see it.

Another fish story was that Papa and the older boys would drive up to Bull Run a small river where two battles were fought during the Civil War. I tagged along several times to witness them find a deep hole in the stream, a "wash" out so to speak, this is where the fish would gather. Papa would take a stick or two of dynamite with cap and fuse, light the fuse and toss it into the deep water. After the explosion the stunned or dead fish would come to the top. Sometimes a snake or two would rise also. There would be eels, catfish, suckers, bass, and sun perch that would be scooped out of the water and taken home, we would have fresh fish for a week.

Another joy of my youth was that I was allowed several dollars to purchase firecrackers at the Fourth of July and strangely enough, also at Christmas. To ignite the wick of the firecracker I would find a locust tree that produced a substance that we referred to as "Punk" or a toad stool. This material would burn in a simmer stage and upon blowing on it, it would glow, therefore allowing me to touch the wick of the firecracker to the glow causing an explosion upon tossing it away. Sometimes I would place the firecracker under a tin can and blow it apart or skyward, another trick was to toss the fire cracker in a neighbors mail box and run.

I also attended several Ku Klux Klan meetings with my Papa, they were usually held on the old Fairfax County fairgrounds. Some of the men would be on horseback with white hoods. I guess this was to be a learning experience. At times they would burn a cross on the front lawn of a neighbor, don't really know why, unless they were sending a message.

For refrigeration we had an ice box. Someone would have to go to the local town and buy a block of ice which was inserted in the top of the box. It kept butter, milk, and the like, fresh for a while, but you could run out of ice. There was a pan under the ice section that caught the water from the melting ice. In the older days, I can remember my granddad had one, people had what was known as a "Spring House." It was located near a natural spring, and as the water ran from the spring, it would spill in a trough that carried it into the spring house. A spring house was usually made of mortar, mud, and thick stone. The walls of this building would be from 12 to 20 inches thick. At the floor there was a bed made of boards with side boards. About the size 4 x 8 ft. The water would spill into this bed creating about four to six inches of water. One would place butter crocks, milk containers, and the like in this spring house and the continuous running water would keep the products cool. The one that was at my grandfather's farm is still standing.

"Spring House" in front of Grandfather's home in 1999. Rumor from the old folks is that raiders hid out in this place during their raids on Fairfax.

An old myth that goes, is that when Mosby raided Fairfax that he hid out in the spring house for a few days. This particular spring house is about two hundred yards from where I was born at Waples Mill. It had to have been built in the late 1700's or early 1800's.

After brother Raymond's wife had her first son in 1933, I was 13, they lived with Papa and Mama for about a year. Papa and Ray built a small house up on a hill nearby that Papa owned. It was a small bungalow, but had no well at first, so we had to carry water there also. I got to be a pretty good water carrier after the turkeys and then to brother Ray's. He was in the huckstering business, himself at this time. I worked for him at times in the summer. I can remember on Sundays if it was raining or snowing, Raymond would take me into Washington DC on 9th St. to see the movies. We arrived about 10 am, and for .15 cents you could see movies all day, never the same, sometimes a love story, several westerns, and a mystery. Those were the days. During the westerns, we use to warn the good guy that the bad guy was behind the rocks, we would yell, "look out" Roy, Tom, or whoever the good cowboy was. We would have a candy bar or popcorn. Also, in addition to the movie, we could watch the cockroaches scamper on the floor when the lights came up.

I wish to mention again about the lighting in our house. In the mid thirties, after Papa built on the addition, the kerosene lamp was not enough light for this big room. Papa bought a lamp, that I believe we had to buy a special type of fuel for, and then had to pump air into the base of the lamp that when turned on would allow two mantels to be ignited with a match. These two mantels would give off the light of half dozen kerosene lamps. Boy, were we thrilled. The Waples were the talk of the community. After electricity was installed, Papa had one light put in each room. The wattage of the bulb was so low I could hardly see, but the Waples had electricity. I remember the light in my bedroom had a string hanging down. I would pull the string and try to jump into bed before the light went out.

One time brother Ray and I took a large load of chicken to Washington to sell on the wholesale market. This was usually on a Thursday. Upon arriving, the space where he was to unload was filled, so he backed into a vacant stall adjacent to his buyer. Well, just as we backed in and got out of the truck and walked to the rear of the load, the owners of this space came out and yelled "Hey you country son of a bitch, you can't park here." With this, after my brother hit him, and he went flying through the pane glass pull down overhead door, we never saw him again. But on the next Saturday as we backed into our retail stand and got out of the truck, the cops arrested Raymond. There I was, about 14 years of age with a load of produce to display and sell. This I did, and about ten a.m. Raymond returned. Sometime later he had to go to court, and when the judge, who was a fox hunting friend of our Papa heard the case, he told the man that when this country boy heard those words, it was time to fight, case dismissed.

I guess it was in the early thirties that I left Oakton School and started to Fairfax Elementary. The county had started to run school buses from Vale to Fairfax that went right by my house. The roads were still dirt so sometimes we had to push the bus, if it got stuck going up Hall's hill. I started Fairfax in the 4th grade and became acquainted with some good kids. We all played baseball and developed into a team that when we were in the 7th grade we beat the Fairfax High School Junior Varsity. When we got to high school we became great. We had two smokin pitchers, Butler and Sherwood, the latter being a first cousin. Another cousin Earl Legge played third base.

I met a girl at Fairfax Elementary School named Louise, fell in love, but being a small freckled-face boy, had lots of competition. We liked each other all through high school. I use to meet her at the end of a large pasture near the woods and maybe sneak a kiss. She later married an 4-F guy during the war, who became very rich from insurance and investments. Later they moved to California, and he became known as the money man. Louise still claims that I was her first boyfriend, her first love.

At Fairfax Elementary, I believe it was either the 4th or 5th grade I had a teacher named Miss Brown, she was the sweetest lady I ever met, other than Mama. I fell in love with her too.

I played baseball and basketball in high school. We did not have football at my time. In those days the boys were not tall like they are now, but I still didn't make the starting five. I was better at baseball. In my baseball career if I could have had a glove modeled like the present day glove I would not have made the two errors that I made.

During those teenage years I was the only child left. I went to school and helped around the farm. Fed and watered the animals, raised chickens, had a bull and raised potatoes for project in the FFA. I won first place with my potatoes. In those days I would send to Sears and Roebucks for baby chicks. They were delivered by the mailman in a cardboard box with small holes in it. I would loose a few, but out of 200 I would raise 190 or so. I had a chicken house with straw on the floor and a brooder heater in the middle of the floor for heat. It took 12 weeks in those days to get a 3 lb. chicken, now Perdue does it in four or five.

My last year that I raised potatoes I made an agreement with the local general store owner that I'd sell all my potatoes to him at harvest for $1.00 per bushel. He agreed, and on the delivery he lived up to his promise. At that time he could have bought them for .60 cents per bushel in Washington, deep in the heart I believe he was being nice to this country boy. I received an "A" on this project.

There was a swimming hole and I learned to swim at an early age. We swam all summer when not doing chores on the farm. The older boys had dammed Difficult Run up at the old fox mill dam using large boulders and smaller stones to do so. The creek at this point had high banks on one side so the location was called "High Banks" by visitors, but to the local boys it was just a swimming hole. We would dive into the water from this bank of about 10 feet high or from a

51

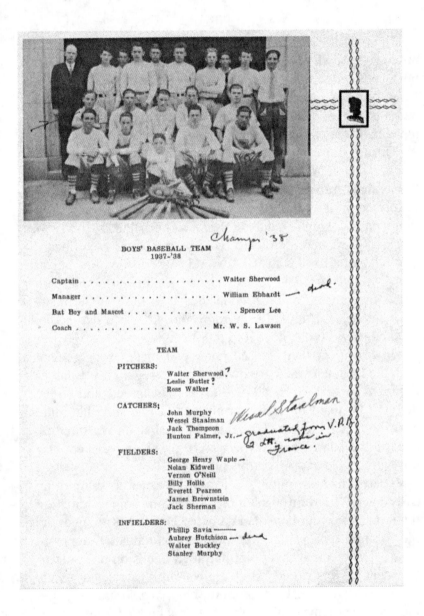

Champ '38

BOYS' BASEBALL TEAM
1937-'38

Captain . . . . Walter Sherwood
Manager . . . . William Ebhardt — *dead.*
Bat Boy and Mascot . . . . Spencer Lee
Coach . . . . Mr. W. S. Lawson

TEAM

PITCHERS:
  Walter Sherwood.?
  Leslie Butler ?
  Ross Walker

CATCHERS:
  John Murphy
  Wessel Staalman   *Wessel Staalman*
  Jack Thompson
  Hunton Palmer, Jr. — *graduated from V.P.I.*
  a Lt. woke in France.

FIELDERS:
  George Henry Waple —
  Nolan Kidwell
  Vernon O'Neill
  Billy Hollis
  Everett Pearson
  James Brownstein
  Jack Sherman

INFIELDERS:
  Phillip Savia ———
  Aubrey Hutchison — *dead*
  Walter Buckley
  Stanley Murphy

Fairfax High School   *Fairfax* County

This is to certify

That **George Waple**

has satisfactorily completed the following Supervised Farm Practice Program

for the Session 1935 - 1936

Enterprises	Supplementary farm jobs
Chicks	Satisfactory
Potatoes	

Given at *Fairfax* District , this *17th* day of *March* 19 3 7

Gordon E. Smith Principal

W. R. Crabill Teacher of Agriculture

Fairfax High School   *Fairfax* County

This is to certify

That *George H Waple*

has satisfactorily completed the following Supervised Farm Practice Program

for the Session 1936 - 1937

Enterprises	Supplementary farm jobs
Chickens 300	Planting Strawberries
Potatoes 1/4 A	Pruning grape vines

Given at *Fairfax Va* District , this *24th* day of *March* 19 3 8

Gordon E. Smith Principal

S H Copeland Teacher of Agriculture

sycamore tree that grew there. We put ladder rungs up the tree and dove from the rung or from the limb that grew out over the water. That sycamore tree is still there, but due to high water, the root system is weak allowing the tree to lean out over the creek. I got to know that ol' tree pretty good and as I drive by today the white limbs wave as to state, "Hi, George Henry." The water at its deepest was about five feet deep. It's a wonder we didn't kill ourselves. What great summer days we had there. If no girls were present we would skinny dip. During a nice hot summer day there would be any where from four to twenty people there. We would play ball, tag, and chase the "chicks" if any were around. One naughty thing we use to do was nab the soda truck as it drove by once a week. There was a steep hill it had to go up and would shift down to a slow speed. On the pass side there was no mirror so we would run along side the truck and each would take all the soda pop he could carry, usually enough to last a day or two. During the summer we would also raid a local watermelon patch, putting the watermelon in the water to cool off. What fun I had in those days, during the 1930's, if all the farm chores were done.

My daily routine during the school year was get up about six o'clock a.m., on my father's command, as he had to walk through my room to get to the stairway. We would milk the two cows then I would feed the other animals, horses, pigs, or whatever. Then I would return to the kitchen, wash up, comb my hair, and by this time Mama had breakfast ready. I would have eggs, hot cakes, oatmeal, bacon or a variety of other things. Papa would say, that oatmeal will stick to your ribs, boy. He was always on me about not cleaning my plate. He would say to my ma, Nannie, "Ain't you gonna make that boy eat the food on his plate?" Mama's reply would be,

George skating on pond that Papa built in the '30's. Behind George is the barn where we milked the cows morning and night.

"Don't worry, what George Henry don't eat your fox hounds will," end of story.

Papa would eat anything and everything. He would suck the marrow from the chicken leg bones, clean everything from his plate with a slice of bread or biscuits by sopping it around his plate. I can see him doing that to this day. He would then push his chair back and light up a Camel or Chesterfield. In those days, they sold for fifteen cents per pack, two packs for a quarter. When the Depression came, he switched to Wings, they were ten cents a pack, saved two and a half cents.

As I've stated, we ate good. If Mama had made biscuits for the previous supper we would have them to dunk in our coffee. Then I would be off to school. Upon return home I would have to bring wood in for the next day, help milk and feed the animals.

In the winter I would carry a lantern for light, as I was always afraid of the dark. It would be scary as I swung the lantern to and fro casting my shadow back and forth, crazy, but true. I was always apprehensive about climbing into the loft thinking that a stranger would be sleeping there. However, it was always comforting when our old gray horse, Pat, would snicker inviting me to his house.

After a good supper I would do my homework, as Papa would go to bed after Amos and Andy. Mama would clean the kitchen and go to bed. When I turned 14 and got my drivers license, Mama bought me a 1929 Chevy Coupe with a rumble seat. This boy had a car. I believe it cost $75.00 The wood part on each side of the windshield rotted, and when the doors were opened they would drop down on the running board. To correct this I secured the doors by running wire across the top of the windshield, but then had to crawl in through the door windows.

Sometimes the Chin boys would come over and listen to Amos and Andy with Papa. They might sit for a while and go home. Wintertime was the "Pitts" with it getting dark so early. Summer time was great, if it was hot we youngsters would go to the swimming hole until dark. I can remember that in the hottest weather papa would sleep on the linoleum floor in the kitchen, it was cooler. There was no insulation or air condition.

During the long summer evenings Papa would stay up till maybe dark. The Chin boys would come over, maybe some other local farmers and they would sit on the porch of the old storehouse. I would be playing out in the road, throwing stones at objects or over the tall maple tree nearby. Papa and his friends would sit there talking about their respective crops or about their animals. How much their team could pull or how much milk ol'bessie the cow gave.

In the attic of the old storehouse I raised pigeons. I had with Papa's help cut a hole in the front end of the building just below the peak of the roof the size of about 2x3 feet. In the evenings the flock of birds that been out feeding all day around the country returned to their roost. They would come in very fast and go directly into the hole we had cut for them. They would nest in the attic and hatch their babies, for which I would fetch, taking the feathers and fuzz off, then sell them at the market for twenty five cents each. Baby pigeons were called squabs, as I recall.

After all of my brothers and sisters had left home, I had my own room. If I had to urinate during the night I would do so by doing it out the back window. After years of this, there was a rust area down the tin roof that was over the back porch, also the acid from the urine would eat a hole in the old sliding screen that was in the window. I can remember that in the summer time, when the windows were open, I could hear bull frogs making their "burr rump" from the pond Papa had made. I loved those sounds, the whippoorwill sing its mating call, that was country. As the song goes, "I was country when country wasn't cool." There were always lots of birds around. The mocking bird being my favorite. What beautiful music it sang, and would sing all night during a full moon. The English Sparrow "Chirp" was also a great sound to me. During the war when we would occupy a farm, usually the barns had vines growing upon them and the sparrow songs reminded me so much of home in Virginia. Even to this day, as I write, I feed hundreds of them in my backyard. Their noises give me a real homey feeling, I love their music. In the fall of the year, when the geese and duck starting migrating, I would sit and watch. Sometimes at night I could hear them fly over. Once in a while a goose or duck would land on the pond. I would get my 410 shotgun, and if I could sneak up on it, and if lucky, we'd have duck for supper.

Mama's brother, Uncle Jack, had a son named Hammond. He was a year or so older than I, but we were playmates. Sometimes I would sleep over and when it rained the water from the upper roof would spill down onto the porch roof which was covered with tin. I loved to hear that sound of rain hitting the tin, it was so comforting.

Once when I had stayed for supper, I planned to return home which was a mile and a half away. As it was raining, I borrowed an old raincoat with a belt around the waist. I did not fasten the belt letting the ends fall to the side. I was walking fast and began to hear a strange noise behind me. Scared to look back, I started to trot, as I trotted the louder the noise became. I then started to run, the noise became louder again, soon I was racing, almost ran myself to death. That damn noise stayed behind me all the way home. I was so glad to reach the back porch when the noise stopped. I then realized the noise was from the belt buckle hitting the side of my rain coat. I sure was glad to be home, really thought the boogie man had me.

I wish to mention something about parents and children. As loving and sweet as Mama was, I don't remember ever seeing Papa hug or kiss one of us. That is until one time when I was about ten. Papa's brother, Uncle Marshall, lived in Washington DC and was doing well for himself in the real-estate business. His son was a city boy and his father knew it. So this one summer, Sunday, when Uncle Marshall had been to the country visiting his older sister and brothers, he stopped by our house to say hello to my Papa. When he was ready to leave he asked if I would like to go home with him and spend a week with his boy, Marshall Jr., I was delighted. Mama gave me some clothes and I was ready to go, and just as I was about ready to enter the car, Uncle Marshall said, "Aren't you going to kiss your Papa good bye," Papa and I kissed. The only time I ever saw him give any of us kids a kiss.

As I've thought about this moment for years I realize why Uncle Marshall asked me to go, he wanted some of my country to rub off on his son. His son became a vet in Alexandria, Virginia. He inherited a bunch of land and money, and today is a wealthy man. I should've stayed with him.

After I got my driver's license, I would drive Papa and Mama wherever they wanted to go. I would get off the school bus each Friday and Mama would be waiting for me to take her food shopping either up to Mr. Dove's general store or to Vienna to the grocery store, like a super market. Papa would give her $5.00 for groceries and a bag of feed for the two cows. Mama would only have to buy the necessary condiments like salt, pepper, sugar, jar jelly, and maybe a loaf of bread for my lunch. The rest of the food came from the farm. I could usually have a nickel for a Clark candy bar, boy, I sure loved that bar of candy. Mama loved ice cream, so if we had another nickel to spare she would buy a vanilla ice cream cone. Years later, after I was in the Army at Fort Myer, Virginia, every time I went home I would go by the ice cream store and buy Mama a quart of vanilla. She could eat the whole quart. I would stand behind her and brush her long grayish hair. Boy, did I love my Mama. She had a mole between her breasts that all of the children fondled with when nursing. After I was grown, and as I would be brushing her hair, I'd say Mama can I play with that mole? She would say, "George Henry, be good, stop that foolishness." I sure loved that lady. I am crying as I write this.

I think I was in the second or third year of high school when Mama sent off to Sears-Roebuck and purchased me a blue surge suit for an upcoming Washington field trip. I remember it was a trifle large with sleeves down over my hands, but she said I'd grow into it. Later after, I joined the Army and hocked this suit on "M" Street, in Georgetown, a dozen times for five dollars. I finally just left it there. If I needed five dollars I would borrow it, returning seven on pay day. On one field trip to Washington we went to the New Auto Show, in those days cars had a stick shift. Before we left the show there was an announcement over the loud speaker for us to return all of the shift knobs as we would be searched on departure. Well, there were knobs all over the place, flower pots, under sofa seats, and light fixtures; we were naughty boys.

Late in the thirties, at the time I was in school, Papa hired a young man named Louis Ellison from Haymarket to chauffeur him. This young man actually went into business with Papa. They would go through the countryside and buy up all they could haul. Papa only had a pickup then. They would prepare the produce for the market, and Louis would take it on Saturday. I would usually go with him to help. We became good friends, and during the summer I would go with him to buy produce. When lunch time came, I'd say, "Louis, I am getting hungry." As we bought some of the produce from country general stores, Louis would have lunch in his pocket after we left the next stop, he was slick.

As I recall, I was about fifteen or sixteen at this time, and knew something about girls. Louis knew two country girls from his neck of the woods. We would save the last two chickens on Saturday afternoon and would go by their apartment and trade the two chickens for companionship.

Papa never went beyond the second grade, but he could read some. When Hitler started making noise in Europe he would read the newspaper and talk about it all of the time.

I do not want to leave a sour impression about my father, even though he drank some and was mean at times, especially when drinking. I don't think we could classify him as being an alcoholic. In the late 30's he quit drinking all together. This man, one could say, was a legend in his own right. In those days, let's say from my memory 1926 on, I have seen Papa display so much kindness, especially to friends and strangers. We had dirt roads and during the winter most were impassable. The mailman even used horse and buggy. Auto traffic was very light and Papa spoke to everyone. If a stranger passed more than once Papa would stop him, introduce himself and ask, "What's your name?" "Where do you live?" I saw you pass the other day. Where are you going?" One time a family rented an old log house that papa had owned and sold. The house was about a quarter mile down the road, but Papa never saw any activity so he went to the door. Here he found a man, wife, and two children, cold with no food. Well, Papa went into action. He went to all of farmers in the entire community gathering up food, whatever the farmer could give, canned products, pieces of pork and meat, and delivered it to this poor family. It seems that the man had been laid off from his job in Washington DC, Papa got him some work around the community until he found a better job. Papa then gave this family a piece of property and helped them to build a house. The man paid Papa back $25.00 per month. I've seen Papa stop a traveler, go through his routine, ask the stranger if he needed potatoes or the like, and if the man said that he did not have any money, Papa would go to the cellar and bring out a 1/2 bushel. Papa helped a lot of people. If any of the neighbors had a sick calf, horse, pig, chickens, Papa was there with his home spun remedy.

As I mentioned, we always ate good, but it's no wonder that Papa died at 62 with heart disease. Mama cooked bacon, mostly fat, then fried eggs in the fat grease or any meat that she had to fry. Then she would use the grease to poor over our pancakes, boy it was good. If any grease was left over, Mama would pour it into a mason jar to preserve it for another meal. Grease or lard as it was referred to from pork sausage was the best. I loved to taste my eggs basted with this lard until the white of the egg became cooked from hot grease.

Something else of interest, in my opinion, if someone had tried to tell Papa that someday there would be a traffic light at the junction of roads 664 and 665 (now known as Fox Mill and Waples Mill Roads) he would have bet his entire bank roll, the whole 12 dollars, that there would never be a traffic light there. If someone drove by going over 15-20 mph, he would stop them and tell them to slow down, they were kicking up too much dust. My father would conduct a traffic survey every day from his perch by the cellar door under the apple tree. This traffic, when it increased to more than several cars a day, was one of the problems, that when added to his heart disease, caused his death. Stress and high blood pressure caused by fast cars and dust, wasn't worth getting sick over.

My Papa, with all of bad times and the good times, was a man who lived beside the road and was a friend of all. If nothing else that I inherited, I am accused to this day for doing more things for other people than I do for my own. Maybe yes or maybe no, but in my book that is not a bad trait, in my opinion.

My father could not render much advice as I left Waples Mill to join the Army, as we never talked much during those early years. I do remember, however, he would preach, ask for no quarter and give no quarter, always use common sense. I don't know where he picked up the following statement, but it always stuck with me. He once told me, "Who you become is what you do for others along the way." This coming from a Papa was a great thought. A couple of other things about my father. In addition to some of his other good points, he was also a weatherman. He could look at the moon and tell if it were a dry or wet moon. If the old Indian Chief could hang his powder horn on the top of the moon, he would stay in his teepee, as it was going to rain. If the chief could not, it was a dry moon and he would go hunting. Papa would state, "you mark my words, it's going to rain before sundown."

The Southern railroad ran just Southwest of Fairfax, heading toward Manassas. If Papa could hear the train whistle he would predict rain. Saying that the atmosphere was low. The wind would be from the south which usually brought wet weather.

In the early thirties the telephone company ran a line or two along Waples Mill Road. Papa took the service, but on our line was maybe four or five other people with each party having a certain number of rings. This was a circus, sometimes when Papa was on the phone, his sister who lived just up the road a piece would pick up her phone to listen in. Papa would yell, "Damn it, Lelia, get off the phone." Of course we would do the same thing, just being nosy or to gain information, this went on for years.

There was a black family who lived on Waples Mill Road, whose name was Jackson. Sometimes when we rode by we would yell unpleasant things at the people hanging out in their yard. Once Mama sent me to Mr. Down's General Store, the man who had bought my potatoes to buy a loaf of bread, and I had to ride by the Jackson house. I was on my bike and as I approached this house I sped up as fast as I could as there was a group of boys and girls playing in the yard. When I got almost to the house, one boy, maybe my age, ten or twelve, ran out into the road and gave me a push. With the bread in one hand, the bike handle began to wobble, and off I went. The road was gravel in those days. I skinned my hands and knees as I fell, but never let loose of the bread. I jumped up and started running toward home leaving my bike. Upon reaching my house I was bleeding, out of breath, and crying. I could say a lot about that incident, but I had better not. One of my older brothers went back and retrieved my bike, and it wasn't long after that when Papa bought Mrs. Jackson's home and land for a song. This property ran along Waples Mill Road for about a half mile. Papa gave brother Raymond a piece of property and helped him build a larger home, as now Ray had three children, and the first place upon the hill was too small.

He also gave a lot to the poor family that had moved in down the road from our place and helped them build a house. Papa gave a lot to sister Lucy, but she never built. That lot, plus a few others, is now where the National Rifle Association is located. On a few other lots Papa built small bungalows.

In my middle teens I helped my father on the construction of these homes.

He sold the house and lot for twenty five hundred dollars, twenty five down and twenty five a month. This was how to get rich quick. One of those homes still stands today. Other lots have large executive buildings as the NRA built on them. If we had only known and retained all of that property as Minnie Chin has done, we would have all been wealthy, so be it.

Mr. and Mrs. Asford, the original buyers in 1937. I stopped by several years ago and introduced myself. They said, "My Lord, are you George Henry?"

In the summer of 1938, there was a retired sergeant and his family who bought the adjoining farm from Papa's sister. The Sergeant had two daughters and two sons. I fell in love with one of the daughters, but she was a complete lady. The

Sergeant's wife was French from W.W.I, and she had a sister who had married another Sergeant after the war, and in 1938 was in the ROTC Unit, at Harvard University. They had a son named Marcel John Newman, who came to visit the Sergeant Mottern who had bought the farm from my Aunt, papa's sister. We became good buddies.

During that summer we had fun. Marcel, his cousins, and I became very close. We would swim, walk two or three miles in the evening to Camp Washington, a cross road of 29-211 and Route 50 near Fairfax Court House, have a soda pop, and listen to the juke box.

Marcel had just finished high school at Cambridge, Massachusetts, and had plans to join the Army at Fort Myer, Virginia, home of the 3rd Horse Cavalry. On the 15th of August he enlisted. We had become good friends and he kept asking me to join the 3rd Cavalry with him. I was only 17 years of age and had not completed high school, had one more year to go. My father and mother finally said OK, and with Papa stating, "You might just as well, you're not going to amount to a hill of beans anyhow." Five days later, on August 20th, I too joined the 3rd Cavalry at Fort Myer, Virginia, with my friend in HQ Troop. As I was only 17, I had to lie about my age and get permission from the County Sheriff as having a clean record. When I joined the 3rd Cavalry at Ft. Myer, Colonel Jonathan Wainwright was Commanding Officer of Fort Myer, that housed 3rd Cavalry and one Battalion of 16th Field Artillery. Around a year or so later, Colonel Wainwright was relieved by Colonel George Patton, who commanded the Third Cavalry from September 1938 to July 1940.

After this Sergeant bought my Aunt's house, where I met Marcel, another retired Sergeant from Fort Myer bought the original house where Papa and Mama lived after marriage.

He was General Pershing's orderly, and brought two beautiful horses with him that belonged to the General. He was a smart looking individual and when he would exercise the horses he would either ride them each or ride one and lead one.

Naturally, at that time, no one knew who General Pershing was or had been. Master Sergeant Smith was still on active duty and dressed in uniform of the day. I remember how neat and soldierly he appeared as he rode by our house, riding one and leading the other. We would say, "There goes Sergeant Smith with General Pershing's horses. We became acquainted and friends; one day he asked me if I could ride, my reply was yes. He then stated, "Come up to my house tomorrow and you can help me exercise the horses." I was thrilled and the next morning I was up bright and early to eat and ride my bike up the road to his house. Sergeant Smith helped me saddle and bridle one horse and warned me of the horse's habits. I mounted and away we went. It is hard to believe at this date that I had become friend to General John J. Pershing's orderly and have ridden the two horses that the Supreme Commander of WWI once rode before he became ill. This was probably my first brush with history.

Just think, here we had General Pershing's horses at Waple's Mill, and at that time this country boy had no idea that he would be in charge of General Pershing's funeral, and be the #1 pallbearer. I still own those white gloves I wore, they hang on my Cavalry sword under my fireplace mantel.

After I got to know Sgt. Smith I would go up to his house before he would exercise the horses. He taught me how to saddle and bridle the mounts military style. He taught me how to hold the reins prior to mounting and how to mount. He taught me how to sit, put heels down in the stirrup, all military style. This all came in handy when I joined the Third Horse Cavalry, August 20, 1938.

Master Sergeant Mottern, Marcel's Uncle, told my parents how great the Army was. After thirty years one could attain the rank of Master Sergeant that rendered a livable retirement. By the time my parents and I received all of this propaganda I was ready, give me a horse and gun, and let me ride. Something I already knew how to do, but did have to learn to do so military style. To join the 3rd Cavalry at that time, we had to get special permission as the unit's table of organization was up to strength. Thanks to the help of a special services hostess, Miss Naylor, who knew Colonel Wainwright very well, we got permission to join.

I played on a sand lot baseball team around the area and Marcel was an addition to the team as he was a catcher back in high school. I pitched most of the games so we became quite a battery. I could throw a roundhouse that broke a foot or so. It was tough to hit. My brother Raymond had taught me that pitch. In August it was all over. Now we were playing soldier for the US Army Third Horse Cavalry.

Radio operator, HQ Troop, 3rd Horse Cavalry

F Troop, 3rd Cavalry, Fort Myer, Virginia

George astride a "mock" horse used for training purposes, in the Caisson Stable, Fort Myer, Virginia

home leave

Cavalry to Infantry:

Enlisted in the Third Cavalry and serviced under Colonel Jonathan Wainright and Colonel George S. Patton prepared George H. Waple for radio communication and leadership roles in the European War as First Sergeant Regimental, HQ 331st Infantry Regiment, 83rd Infantry Divisions.

Platoon Sergeant
3rd   Cavalry

Mounted on "Rusty"

Scout Car Platoon 3rd Cavalry

73

BOOTS AND SADDLES

3rd US Cavalry

I took basic training along with my friend, Newman, under the guidance of Corporal White. He was a fine looking man, tall, lean, and smart. Corporal White had been in the Third Cavalry for six years. He took Newman and me under his wing and taught us basic training, such as military courtesy, the salute, proper dress, and horsemanship. He taught us how to polish our equipment, and maintain our saddle and bridle. We slept next to Corporal White in a large squad room. The army cots were about two feet apart with a footlocker at the head or foot of the bed, as the case demanded. The locker had to be neat at all times.

The other soldiers were mostly old-timers, some whom had found a home in the Army. Under Corporal White's tutelage we became soldiers quickly, but were harassed constantly by the old troopers. One time we were short sheeted and sent to the supply room for new sheets, and were told there were no sheets, then sent to the next barracks for the sheets, and once again, there were no sheets.

When we would ride with the troop, the old soldiers would yell at Newman and me, "Hey Recruit, keep those spurs out of the horse's ears." In the Cavalry a trooper is supposed to keep his heels pointing down. Newman was new at riding and soon developed a saddle sore on his tail bone, but had too much pride to report to sick call. I went to the stable Sergeant and got some salve and ointment used on horses and doctored him. He had evidence of that sore for many years.

One day after lunch, I strolled by the room of our supply Sgt., Sgt. Thomas. The door was open and he was napping, so I thought, with a cigar in his mouth and ashes falling on his chest. I hesitated, but finally went into his room, tapping him on his left shoulder, saying, Sgt. Thomas, your cigar ashes are falling on your chest. With this, not removing the cigar, he said out of the corner of his mouth, "Look, recruit, I've been doing this for twenty years, Now get outa' here."

Another time I went into the day room to watch a poker game. As Sgt. Thomas's back was toward me, I could see a dollar bill lying on the floor near his chair. I walked in and placed my left foot on top of the dollar. Without looking up, he said, "Recruit, if you don't want a broken leg, get your foot off that dollar." I turned and left quickly. He and I became buddies as time went on.

Upon enlisting I was told to get a hair cut. I reported to the main Post Exchange Building and was told to go upstairs and would see the barber pole. I had never had a store bought hair cut before, and when the barber told me where to sit, I said to him, "if I sit there, where are you going to sit?" You see, I thought I was to sit where one would normally place his feet. The barber was astonished and asked, "where are you from boy?"

It was also about this time that I bought an ice cream cone in the Post Exchange. As I was leaving the building, I met my Troop Commander. When I saluted I was told to get rid of the ice cream, as no trooper under his command was going to walk around with an ice cream cone in his hand. I was told, go get a beer trooper.

I started smoking soon after joining the Army, probable for no other reason than trying to be a big shot. I smoked "Taylor Made" or store bought cigarettes at that time, and upon lighting up, if among the troopers, I would hear the word "Butts" which meant that after several drags another trooper wanted what was left. Sometimes there would be a "second" to the first "Butts." Most of the old soldiers smoked, roll your own, i.e., Bull Durham. It was fascinating to see the First Sergeant take his bag of Bull Durham, while mounted, open the bag with his teeth, hold the thin paper in his rein hand, poor the tobacco in the paper, lick, and then fold into a cigarette. I never learned this trick, although I tried, so I too could do like the old timers.

One day on my way home all dressed up in my class "A" uniform, which consisted of shirt, tie, blouse, belt, breeches, and boots with spurs, everything polished and I thought I looked good. En route home, I stopped by my former high school. As I strolled down the hall I was met by Mr. Smith, the principal. He was astonished and more or less shouted at me, saying, "What in the *hell* have you done? You joined the Army? Why? You're in there with all of those bums and why are you here?" My reply after a second or two was I wanted to visit some of my classmates. With this he said, "Ok, but then be on your way."

About two months after enlisting, Newman and I had learned enough about soldiering that we joined the squadron consisting of our Troop, MG Troop, and E & F Troops on an extended march through the Maryland countryside ending up at Fort Meade, Maryland. On the first night out we bivouacked somewhere in the countryside by a stream, in Maryland. Corporal White had taught us how to pitch our "pup" tent, and got us bedded down. The horses were taken care of and tied to the picket line about forty feet in front of our row of tents. There always had to be a "picket line" guard.

Someone had to untangle the horses in case they got "spooked." The old soldiers who were taking turns on guard had talked it over among themselves and at about midnight we got a call, "Waple/Newman," (it was always Waple/Newman, never Newman/Waple for some reason) "Wakeup, wake up, piss call, piss call, didn't you hear the bugle, everyone has to get up at midnight and go to the latrine, you're late, don't go to the latrine now, just go out by the picket line and take a leak." That we did, and back to our tent. The next day we heard that from everyone, "Hey, Waple/Newman, did you make "piss call" last night?" It was the joke of the day.

Another time Newman, my recruit friend, was assigned picket line guard. This job was to walk around the horse picket line, note that none were tangled and count them. As Marcel made one trip around counting the horses by the light of a lantern, he counted 56, the next time it was 52. Being a recruit he became excited, sat the lantern down and started counting again, very carefully. When he made the full trip around the picket line he counted 62 and in reaching the spot where he sat the lantern down it was gone. With this he called "Corporal of the Guard" as he was very upset. What happened was that two or three old soldiers were playing a trick on him. The next day he was the laughing stock of the troop. "Hey Newman, how many horses you got?" He and I had out butts ridden off by the older troopers. We were just babies to them, but it was all in fun. They really treated us good, always giving us tips on how to make the grade. Being a horse soldier, a member of the 3rd Cavalry was an honor. We were in a proud unit. The 3rd Cavalry wore the brave rifle insignia, and our motto was "Trooper of the 3rd Cavalry you have been baptized in blood and fire and came out men of steel."

We were on that trip about ten days, playing soldier and command post exercises, returning to Fort Myer without incident. In fact, we did so good under the guidance of Corporal White, that upon return, our troop Commander, Capt. Trapnell, who later retired as a Lieutenant General, promoted us both to Sixth Class Specialist, a three dollar per month raise.

In those days, a private was paid $21.00 per month, a fee of $1.50 per month was taken out for laundry, and a few cents for the old soldiers home. After this, if one smoked, and by the time you bought your toiletries, there was only a few dollars left. So after the first week of the month one was broke and stayed in the barracks until the next pay day, unless he just wanted to take a walk.

We could buy post exchange coupons, $2.00 or $5.00 book, plus a movie theater book for a few dollars. Some of us who could manage our few dollars could buy a $5.00 book of coupons for $3.00 cash, as the seller was looking for cash, so that he could go to town and have a ball. We could go to Washington, DC for five cents, on the bus. If one had thirty five cents, they could go to town and buy three white tower hamburgers, coffee or milk, and a piece of pie, total .25 cents, with a nickel to spare for bus ride back to the Fort. Lots of times we would pan handle on the streets for bus fare back, and if you got .15 cents you could buy a beer, then go back and beg for bus fare back home. Soldiers did not have the best reputation in those pre-war years. For instance, in Lafayette Square, near the White House, I remember there was a sign posted, "No soldiers or dogs allowed." All of this changed later after Pearl Harbor. We then all of a sudden became heros.

Another duty I performed was regular guard duty. There were about twelve or so areas that needed to be guarded throughout the Fort. At four thirty every day there would be guard mount where all of the men would gather, be inspected, and assigned their respective post for the night. One of the group of thirty or so would be selected to be the Colonel's orderly the next day. This man could return to his barracks with instructions to report to the regimental adjutant the next morning at seven thirty. Everyone bucked for this job as there was nothing for him to do all day except run errands. To be selected to this task was not easy. Only the best dressed, best polished, cleanest side arm, and knowledge of the chain of command from the President on down to the Post Commander would be picked. Every soldier was given a number when he enlisted, mine was twelve. This number had to be stenciled on every item of clothing and all the equipment he possessed. Sometimes the officer of the day would ask to see your handkerchief or something else if the inspection was a tie. He would eventually find the orderly.

When I noticed that I was to perform guard duty the next day, I started preparing at noon. If one was to pull the duty they were dismissed from all other chores at noon of that day. My uniform was pressed, leather polished, pistol clean, and a close shave, and hair cut. We wore boots, breeches, shirt, tie, and blouse. All had to be perfect. When I put on my breeches I would not pull them all the way up, I would put on my boots and tie them next, and finally pull up my breeches making them skin tight without a wrinkle. Then I finished dressing usually with help of another trooper. I would walk stiff legged down the stairway and to the guardhouse. Sometimes I would have two other troopers carry me down the stairs so as not to bend your knee. After I had done this chore several times I usually would be selected as the

79

colonel's orderly. I did not particularly care to walk guard duty. Some guard posts were in isolated areas, and as I stated earlier, I was always afraid of the dark. Also, the officer of the day would normally visit once during my tour. I had to challenge him by yelling, "Halt, who goes there?" The response was supposed to be, "Officer of the Day." I then would command, "Advanced to be recognized" and as he did, I would then command, "Halt," and state, "Officer of the Day recognized." He then would ask questions such as where does your post extend? Repeat several of the eleven "General Orders" that every soldier had to know, and if there were any special orders, he would ask what they were. A young soldier had to be on his toes because if the Officer of the Day wasn't satisfied with the answers, the soldiers would be relieved and in deep trouble. I was never relieved from any duty. In fact, and I'll state it now for the record, I never missed a formation in my entire career. I never received any extra duty or was denied a privilege.

One time, I witnessed my recruit instructor, Corporal White, give an extra K.P. to a soldier who was a wise guy. The man stated back to Corporal White, "Why don't you make it two?" Before this discussion was over that soldier was on KP every weekend for the rest of his enlistment. It was a good thing W.W.II came along in his behalf.

Corporal White's enlistment was up in 1941. He left the Cavalry for a more exciting position with the Air Force. Later I heard that he had been killed serving as a tail gunner of a B-17.

For a military occupation I took up radio operating and learned the Morse code easily. We had a radio room in the barracks where we trained, but for field communications we had a hand cranked horse mounted radio with a knee key for transmitting. After I got proficient in this task I received a promotion which gave me another three dollar raise in pay. I believe I was now making twenty-seven dollars per month.

After a year, because of my attention to duty, as the First Sergeant put it, I was assigned by the "Top" to become the Troop Commander's orderly while his regular orderly was on furlough. I did not relish this job, as I did not want to be a "dog robber." However, there was no way to fight the assignment. I would get up early, eat early chow, and go to the stables alone. I would saddle the Captain's horse and be ready when he showed up. I would hold his mount as he mounted, then I would mount. One day after several weeks of this he and I went to the riding hall ahead of the troops. The captain loved to whistle, did so most of the time. All of a sudden he stopped whistling and announced, in a clear sharp command, "Private Waple," I see fit to promote you to Private First Class," and started whistling again. I was happy as a "Peacock." I now would make thirty-six dollars per month, Hooray. Later, as the special order was posted on the bulletin board reflecting my promotion, I really took a razzing from the old soldiers, some of whom had served much longer than I. They called me "ass kisser," and about everything else they could think of. I was very happy and called my Mama soon to tell her. Of course she did not understand, but praised her baby boy.

One aspect of this orderly job was in the afternoon I had to report to the Captain's quarters. I would polish his boots, sam brown, belt, and brass. This wasn't too bad, but then if the Captain's wife wanted me to polish silver, wash windows, or another menial task, I had to do so. I felt that I did not join the Army to become a servant. The job did pay five dollars per month extra. On the brighter side, however, there were times when the Captain and his lady would be away. I would be on my own to exercise the two horses that were assigned to him. One was named Rusty, the other Meadow Brook. Rusty was a jumper and could fly. I would go to the parade field where jumps were located and copy the steeple chase racing I had seen in upper Virginia. Rusty was a great gelding. Now for the mare, she was beautiful. She could also jump, but with more class than Rusty. She could cantor beautifully, and change leads on rein commands. At slow canter it was like sitting in a rocking chair. I would sit there with the seat of my breeches never leaving the saddle. The mare would comply with the reins touching her neck. It was fun performing a figure eight.

I would pretend that I was riding in the National Horse Show. This mare could do it all, trot sideways, back up on leg command, stop, and go forward on leg command. She would stop on a "WHOA," move on a "cluck." She was a joy to ride. I really took good care of those two mounts. I would have the fantasy of being a country gentlemen doing his thing in the show ring, sit up right, heels down, legs in, and hands proper, I loved it.

Sometimes, on Rusty, I would have a fantasy of being a great jockey as I would gallop around the horse exercise field. I would sit a little sideways, shorten one rein, and let him rip, I was in heaven. He could really jump going into a high fence, and just before his take off, I would yell, "Yaugh." Rusty was only about fourteen hands if that, but he could go.

On regular duty I was assigned a beautiful black mare. I've forgotten her name, but she was "Black Beauty" to me, she could also jump. A rider and his horse soon learned each others feelings, I learned when she was ready to take off. I would stand tall in the saddle, taking all of my weight off her, it was like flying for a moment, great sport. Once when I was riding this mare in the riding hall there were three jumps on each side, and about four feet in height. I was practicing a special ride that my troop performed in a special horse show for the Washington High Society.

I would be with seven other riders, two in each corner. On the last event I would be without saddle or bridle, just me and my mount. We would circle the hall taking the jump at a racing speed, the band would play as we raced, and at the end of the ride the horses headed for the exit. Outside was a tarp to stop them. I was last, and we were flying, but instead of my mare taking the last jump as I expected, she cut and sped for the exit after the fifth jump. As all I had was legs on her abrupt turn, I slid off, as I put my arm down to break my fall upon hitting the tan bark my wrist snapped. The mare kicked his heels high as if to say, "Ha ha, I sure fooled you, didn't I." I was on the Disabled List for a while.

Each troop of the Third Cavalry and each Battery of the 16th Field Artillery had a special event they would perform during the horse shows. My troop, in addition to the event mentioned earlier was a "Bridleless Ride" exercise. As a troop, we would ride into the hall, form a line facing the audience and render a salute. We would then reach over and remove the bridle from the horse's head. At this point, the band would start the music. As a result of rehearsals, the horses responded, we would form a column of fours and go through a complete routine guiding the horse with our legs and breast strap, it was quite amazing. On the subject of the Sixteenth Field Artillery, there was a young man who joined the unit during the mid thirties who went by the name of Forrest Tucker, who was a handsome dude and was discovered by someone in Washington as being a candidate for the movies. He was six foot or so and had blonde hair. He left the artillery about the time that I joined the Third

Cavalry. I only met him once, as there was a young lady, Hughette Mottern, who was a friend of his and later became a friend of mine. Mr. Tucker went onto stardom.

In addition to the Third Cavalry and Sixteenth Field Artillery, there was a troop of black soldiers of the Tenth Cavalry. They were great and had a ride of their own, real horsemanship and spit and polish. They were good soldiers and performed beautifully. I am sorry I did not get to know them better as I know I should have now.

I recall my first baptism in a drinking spree with the old soldiers. We would chip in and buy several quarts of gin, get a large aluminum coffee pitcher, and then steal several quarts of grapefruit juice from the kitchen. We would pour all of this in the pitcher, mix, and sit in a circle on footlockers and pass the pitcher. This was my first time to get drunk. As the pitcher made the circle, it did not take long for me to feel the room spin. They put me to bed with a G.I. can beside me. Sure enough they were right, It wasn't long before I was sicker than a hound dog. I threw up all night, but made reveille the next morning.

We were awakened by a whistle blown by the charge of quarters fifteen minutes before we had to fall out in front of the barracks for reveille. In the winter time, some of the older troopers would stay in bed till the whistle blew again signaling us to go outside. They would then jump out of bed, slip on their boots, and overcoat, nothing else. I remember one time the First Sergeant commanded us to remove our overcoats, with this, there were about ten men in their shorts. He made these troopers do double time around the parade field in their skivvies, it was funny as hell. At other times, the 1st Sergeant would command us to raise our arms over head. At this time, one could see cigarette sparks flying through the air as the troopers dropped cigarettes from their cupped hands.

It may have been during the winter of 1938 or 1939 when I accompanied Newman to his home in Cambridge, Massachusetts on a Greyhound bus. His parents lived on the bank of the Charles River with Harvard just across the way. The river was frozen and we would skate. I wasn't very good, but gave it my best country try. During the evenings we would go to a juke box parlor, have a soda pop, and dance. I wasn't much of a dancer either, but those kids could really "jitter bug" or "lindy hop." I enjoyed watching as the girl's skirts would fly out on the turns. Enroute home to Ft. Myer, when the bus would stop for a rest, we would put a nickel in the jukebox and act really "hip." I couldn't even spell "hip" much less act like it. I watched and caught on, and it wasn't long before I could shake a leg or two.

Learning to shoot the 45-caliber pistol was tough for me. The target would be fifty feet away and was hard to hit. We also had to learn to shoot the pistol from horseback. We were also armed with a sword and had to learn to stab a straw head mounted on a post while riding by on our horse. If you missed the straw and hit the post, it would really jar your arm and shoulder.

When mounted we were armed with the .03 bolt action rifle. To qualify we were trucked to a rifle range in NE Washington DC on the Maryland line. I had shot a 22-caliber rifle many times and shot guns, but never shot a rifle such as this. It had a kick, and if you got too close, the bolt would come back into your nose if not held properly. I did not qualify the first attempt, and to get a badge you must qualify. To get me another try attempt, my coach reached out with a small hammer from the tool box and hit the front sight to make it crooked. He then called the Captain and stated, "No wonder this recruit can't hit the target, the front sight is crooked." With this he was instructed by the Captain to straighten the sight and have me try again. I didn't qualify as an expert, but did become a good enough marksman to qualify for a badge.

All of the Privates had to do kitchen police (KP) and stable police. KP was a chore, but during the cold winter months it was better than going on horse exercise. KP consisted of reporting to the kitchen about five a.m. You would help get the breakfast meal ready and place the food on the table when the meal was to be served. We served family style and had to keep running back and forth from the kitchen to the dining room. Before we got a dish washer and potato peeler, we did these chores manually. After each meal, the tables were cleaned and the floors mopped. There were always lots of pots and pans to do. KP was an all day job. We were finished when the kitchen floor was mopped after the supper meal. One good thing about KP was that you got plenty to eat. Sometimes, if I was broke and going to be around over the weekend, I would do KP for a friend for five dollars.

Stable police was good, we cleaned the stables, stacked hay, and cleaned the stable yard. I loved to be around the horses. The horses had to be exercised daily and our troop had about sixty horses, but for that duty, we may have had twenty or so troopers present for regular duty. Therefore, we would ride one, lead two, and as the Corporals or Sergeants didn't groom, we would groom five or six.

One time during bad weather we were grooming in the stable. I was taking care of the stable Sergeant's horse and cleaning the horses fet locks. This Sergeant was a big German man. He asked, "Waple, did you get my horses fet locks good," "Yes sir," I replied. With this he tested this area behind the horses hoof and found some sand. He picked me up by front of my olive drab shirt and slapped the TAR out of me. As I went back down to do a better job, I was crying. I guess I wondered what I had gotten myself into. It wasn't this bad back on the farm.

I had to keep my saddle and bridle clean and all brass polished. We used saddle soap for the leather and blitz cloth to do the brass, this was a continuous job. My boots, belt, pistol holster, and all uniform brass had to be highly polished at all times. I thought I was pretty nifty when all dressed in my khaki breeches, blouse, and boots. Spurs for the boots too.

It was probably the winter of 1938 that I played on the troop basketball team. Each troop and field artillery battery fielded a team under the Fort intramural league. Our team consisting of only six players, one being a Lieutenant who had attended Georgetown, was pretty good. In fact, the Lieutenant got us a game with the freshman team from Georgetown. We played away, and after the game we decided to visit a former lady friend of the Lieutenant's. No one had any money so I hocked my topcoat for five dollars at a pawnshop on "M" Street. The Lieutenant had the car so we picked the lady up and drove back to Fort Myer and parked in an isolated area with each taking his turn. All of this for five bucks. I don't know in what order we went, but if we went according to rank, I would be last, and if we went in alphabetical order I would be last. However, I should've gone first as it was my coat we pawned.

An incident that has stayed with me forever was at the time I was assigned to be the Captain's orderly and could walk to the stables to get our horses ready prior to the troops arriving, I met a Major who was riding up the street in the stable area. As I approached him I rendered a salute. He responded with his riding crop in his saluting hand and with a pipe in his mouth. Well, one could hear the next sound a mile away, as the Major had just ridden by the entrance of the stable where Colonel George Patton's horses were kept. He had not noticed Colonel Patton exiting the stable as he rode by. Colonel Patton noticed the salute of the Major, riding crop, pipe, and he yelled, "Major, turn around and come back here." He then commanded me to return up the street, and told the Major to give me another salute without crop in hand or pipe in mouth, which he did. I gave him another hand salute, and then saluted Colonel Patton. I felt ten feet tall.

A few months later the First Sergeant called me in the Orderly Room and informed me that I would fill in for Colonel Patton's regular orderly for a month. He told me our Troop Commander, for whom I'd worked a few months, had recommended me. What could I say, even though I didn't like to be a "dog robber," slang for orderly. Being Colonel Patton's orderly was different; I came to know the Colonel, Mrs. Patton, and his three children as each morning some of them would ride.

After a short tour with Colonel Patton, I was returned to regular duty, made corporal in a few days with Colonel Patton pinning my Corporal Chevrons on. It was another great moment; Colonel Patton left the 3rd Cavalry to become a great General.

During my early summer days at Fort Myer I also played softball for a team run by my brother Rufus. We played in Washington and all around Northern Virginia. He had hired a pitcher who threw the softball like a bullet. Very few would ever get a hit off of him. Brother Rufus would bet quite a sum of money on these games. Most of the other teams had fast pitchers too, so really what it boiled down to was who had the best pitchers. I usually played infield or any other position. One time, an opposing batter did hit a ground ball, and as the ball and runner reached first base about the same time, the runner reached out and touched my face attempting to distract me. Well, you never saw such a brawl in your life. As the runner did this, he tripped over the base and fell, with this I was immediately on top of him bashing his face. I ended up somehow on the bottom after some scuffling. I had my arms pinned. My cousin Marshall was there as I yelled, "Get him off of me," with this Marshall bit the rascal in the rib cage, he sure did let loose quickly.

When the rumors of war started flying during 1940 and 1941, Washington DC became full of young ladies from all over seeking government work. When we were still allowed to wear civilian clothes, the ladies did not know we were soldiers, those were beautiful days. One could walk in to any cocktail lounge and have a choice. Newman and I would pick out a couple, introduce ourselves, and usually have a nice evening. We would each have a birthday soon if we stayed acquainted a week or so. There would be a party at their place usually on them. On some of those meetings, if I really wanted close companionship, I would pick out a lady not so attractive, as they were usually very appreciative. I had another friend who took his date on a walk through Arlington Cemetery, when we got back together that evening, the lady had an imprint on the back of her dress, "Died 1890."

Most of the ladies found housing in quarters just below Arlington Cemetery. They were furnished by the government, and this area was later called South Post. As the war got closer we had to wear uniforms, and then everyone became patriotic. A soldier couldn't buy a beer, or anything else as a matter of fact. Washington, DC in the spring was as beautiful as it is today. Some Sundays I would take a horse and go for a ride, we could go through the cemetery and around an experimental farm; the area that became the South Post and Pentagon. We didn't have much money, but had food, lodging, and had fun when off duty.

I remember one time my sister Hazel had given me ten dollars. When I took my uniform off to take a shower I laid my wallet, etc. on my bed. When I returned from the shower my wallet was gone. I looked and looked and reported to the charge of quarters that my wallet was stolen. It was on Wednesday or Thursday of the next week that I received in the mail my wallet with all cards, etc., minus the ten dollars from a person who had found it at the beach. I went to the 1st Sergeant and told him, and showed the note and wallet. The top kick called in the NCO's that had been on duty Saturday and Sunday and asked if they had noticed anyone looking like they had been to the beach over the weekend. One NCO immediately stated that he had as he was sitting on the front porch of the barracks Sunday, and PFC Smith had been dropped off and stated that he had been to the beach where the wallet was found. The First Sergeant called Smith to the orderly rooms and confronted him with the evidence. He admitted that he had taken the wallet. I was shocked as Smith was a pal, I thought. I went to his defense, but the Troop Commander said that he had committed a crime against society and would be punished. He got 6 months in the guard house. I don't know what happened to him.

In 1939 Marcel and I bought a 1931 Chevy convertible, yellow with red wheels. He could not drive so I chauffeured. We had lots of chicks and drove out to my home or his Uncle's farm every weekend. His cousin, Hughette, whom I had the hots for, but she was a real good Catholic girl. I do remember kissing her several times. Once she was in the back seat of our car, and pushed the passenger seat forward.

The back of the seat went through the windshield. A few days later our troop Commander noticed the car out front of the barracks and told the top kick to tell us to get it off the post. We then parked it out back by the drug store on Pershing Drive, about four blocks away.

On one of my visits home, after being in the Army for a while my Papa started talking to me. I don't believe that we had ever had a man to man talk before I joined the Army. He owned a six shooter but I don't remember ever seeing him fire it. This visit I had taken a few tracer pistol bullets home with me. I asked him to fetch his pistol for me as I would like to fire it, as I had brought some bullets home with me. I fired a couple of regular rounds and then slipped in some tracer bullets. I had set up a target against a bail of dry straw and asked him if he thought he could hit the target, it was only about fifty feet away. With this he aimed, fired, and when the tracer bullet hit the bail of hay, the bullet started a small fire. He yelled, "What in the hell was that?" He had never seen a tracer bullet much less fire one. I had a good laugh as I explained what had happened. We became buddies for the first time of my life, that was great.

In 1940 I made Corporal, and it was at this time the Department of the Army came out with a regulation stating that anyone who wanted to enlist for one year could do so, and avoid the draft that was to begin in the near future. My troop had 12 of these young men enlist under this clause. Of the 12, there was one man who was about 30 years of age and older than the rest. I was assigned to give these men full recruit training. Just being promoted to Corporal I had to study like hell to learn what I was to teach. Close order drill, manual of arms, and horsemanship was a snap, but gas drill and map reading, I had to study. There was a master training schedule that I had to follow. Another Corporal from the machine gun troop also had a group, so we joined forces and trained together. My group was a great bunch of men. I trained them, slept with them, and ate with them. They were my dirty dozen. The chap that was about thirty and a graduate from a college in Pennsylvania, and the University of Virginia, was a smart dude. He was a banker as I recall, and had a new 1940 Buick Convertible. Not only was I his recruit Corporal, but at night I became his chauffeur. He had the dough, and would take a few of us into Washington, DC where he belonged to the University Club, drinks were on him. We had a blast.

One time he took me to his cousin's house for the weekend in Middleburg, Virginia. The house was a mansion and I'll never forget the hospitality I was given. These people had servants, one couldn't move without someone asking you if you wanted a drink or something else. However, one time during the weekend my friend's cousin and I were walking up the street in Middleburg, and during the conversation he asked me where I had gone to school. I was embarrassed when I had to answer that I had not gone to college, but I didn't tell him I was a high school drop out. Also, when we had a formal dinner that evening I was confused when I saw all of the knives, forks, and spoons, also glasses, how many glasses and utensils does one need? I was smart enough though to watch what other people were doing, so I made it through the dinner OK, I guess. When we left the table and went to the library for cigars and brandy, I am sure I felt that this was class. Sure is funny now that I can reminisce about those days.

After the war, I only met one of those men of the dirty dozen. I ran into him in the Pentagon, he was now a Captain. When I was giving the group their recruit training, this particular young man impressed me as also being one from a class family. He was very neat, learned fast, and as I recall, had been to a private military school.

Once, after I made Corporal, I was put in charge of the jump detail in the riding hall, that's a job to replace the jump poles if knocked down by the jumping horse. One time that happened was when Colonel Patton's daughter was riding over jumps and her horse refused, she went flying over the horse's head and landed on the tan bark, a substance used on the floor of the hall. As one of my troopers ran over to assist her, she yelled "Get your hands off me dog face," a slang name for a soldier in those days. We would see a lot of her riding and she wasn't a very pleasant person. Her brother, George Patton, was about 14 at that time, we would see him around once in a while. I served with him in Korea when he was a Captain. He retired as a Major General, and took up residence in Massachusetts. He later passed on in June 2004.

My first enlistment was completed, I had made Corporal and then Sergeant prior to August 1941. I reenlisted to fill my vacancy, and was sent to Communications School at Ft. Monmouth in the fall of 1941. I was there when the Japanese attacked Pearl Harbor.

While at Communications School one evening I went to the Last Chance Bar in Oceanport. I wore my boots, breeches, and campaign hat, I thought I looked great. When I ordered a beer, I was refused as the bartender thought I was a Boyscout. That bar was torn down later and now it is a park. Finished school in March or February 1942, and returned to Ft. Myer, Virginia. I met a nurse from Long Branch Hospital after arriving at Fort Monmouth. We dated almost every night as she had a car. She was from Farmingdale and I was taken to her home for Thanksgiving dinner November 1941. Her folks were nice, with her mother being a great cook. I impressed her father with my Southern drawl and politeness, i.e., Yes sir, no sir, and the like.

Just after returning to Ft. Myer, the young lady and I discovered that we had fallen in love and missed each other. So with the permission of my troop Commander to get married, and only making $54.00 per month, she came to Washington, DC on the train. I met her at the station, and took her to a brother's home in close by Arlington. By sneaking out on February 15, 1942 we managed to get a blood test, marriage license, a ring from a pawn shop on Ninth Street in Washington for $4.00, and lined up at the Justice of the Peace. On February 16, 1942, we were married. The total cost of entire wedding was $16.00. Marcel was my best man, and my sister Lucy stood up with my wife to be. I got permission to stay out of the barracks on February 16. We stayed at my brother's home in Arlington. After the marriage ceremony we drove out to my home to introduce my new wife to Papa and Mama. Papa, being the sport that he was, gave us a ten-dollar bill for a wedding present, now I was only six dollars in debt. The next day, February 17th, my wife Kitty boarded the train back to New Jersey to work at the hospital. In March, we loaded our horses and equipment on trains and headed to Fort Oglethorpe, Georgia. I, by this time, had transferred from horses to Scout Car Section Chief. The war was on and rumors came that the Horse Cavalry was to be disbanded.

Just before my first enlistment was up I was placed in the Scout Car Platoon that was commanded by Newman. I became a Section Chief and Main Radio Operator. I think we had six scout cars, and for normal training we would set up an exercise primarily for communication experience. Newman would send us off in different directions and I would sometimes drive out to my home at Waples Mill. Papa and Mama were impressed with their son, George Henry, now Sergeant Waple.

Being in the Scout Car Platoon, now we were to drive to Fort Oglethrope in convoy with all of the equipment gone with the horses. We were all packed and ready to roll the next morning early. The night before a group of us went to Washington DC and tied one on. It seems, however, that the next morning early I was one of a few who could still soldier. Marcel was passed out, so I hid him in the back of my scout car. When the Captain was getting the Convoy ready to roll, he kept looking for Newman. I would tell him that he just went that way. The Captain never found Newman, and I am glad, because I believe he would have been a Private soon. Newman never forgot this deed of mine and whenever he could, he always looked out for me. We were buddies to say the least and remained that way the entire war.

After arriving at Ft. Oglethrope we did the usual training and horse exercise. It was mid summer that a Cadre would be picked from the 3rd Cavalry and sent to the Infantry. We had been at Fort Oglethrope, Georgia, from March 1942 through June.

My wife joined me for a while in Georgia. I had gotten a one room (living and bedroom) with a closet and a kitchen for $30.00 per month, I was earning $54.00. My wife, who was a registered nurse, could not find a job in Chattanooga, TN as a nurse, so she took a job in the "Hash House," by the street car and bus barns. She would walk about eight blocks with me to catch a bus to camp, and she would go to work in the restaurant at 5 a.m. for one dollar per day, plus tips. She made four or five dollars a day. It was really the "pits," but we survived. When I left Georgia for Indiana, my wife returned to New Jersey and to her regular job as a nurse in Long Branch.

When I left the 3rd Cavalry, I was headed for the Infantry. I managed to keep my campaign hat, my original mess kit, the one that had a flat top, and one would have a hell of a time keeping a half a peach on it while walking, I have my spurs and a saber that I used when riding as a mounted color guard. I have a picture of myself as a mounted color guard riding down Pennsylvania Ave. in Washington, DC. When a flyover of airplanes flew past, I looked up at the planes when the picture was taken. I almost was reduced in grade (busted as it was called in those days) over that incident. I should have been looking straight ahead. The picture appeared in the Washington paper which was delivered to my home at Waple's Mill. Mama cut it out with pinking sheers and wrote my name by my head. The photo, which is now in the museum at Fort Myer, Virginia, was chosen to be the front cover of the book.

I was promoted to Staff Sergeant and sent to Camp Atterbury, Indiana, along with a 1st Sergeant (who happened to be named J. Newman) supply, mess, and platoon Sergeants. I was Radio Chief of the Communication Platoon. After arriving at Atterbury, getting settled in, our "fillers," draftees and enlistees started arriving from enlistment centers and other assignments. The entire 83rd Division soon became full strength.

I often wonder what happened to the beautiful horses after the Third Cavalry was disbanded. They were probably sold at an auction to riding stables or individuals. Whoever got Meadowbrook, Rusty, and my Black Beauty received outstanding animals.

First Sergeant Waple

Capt. Whitney and 1st Sergeant Waple, Camp Atterbury Indiana 1943

"Short arm" inspection

1st Sergeant Waple, 331st Infantry – 83rd Division

GEORGE HENRY WAPLE III

8 FEB 1921 – ()

ENLISTED IN THIRD HORSE CAVALRY FORT MYER, VIRGINIA 20 AUGUST 1938. ASSIGNED TO 83RD I.D. JUNE 1942. PROMOTED TO MASTER SERGEANT AT AGE 21 NOVEMBER 1942. AS FIRST SGT. OF 331ST INFANTRY, 83 ID PARTICIPATED IN ALL CAMPAIGNS FROM NORMANDY TO THE ELBE RIVER. RECEIVED THE "COMBAT INFANTRY BADGE" AND TWO "BRONZE STARS" FOR THE FIVE CAMPAIGNS IN EUROPE.

RETURNED TO FT. MYER, NOVEMBER 1945 AS FIRST SERGEANT, CEREMONIAL DETACHMENT LATER TO BECOME "A" COMPANY, 3RD INFANTRY 5 APRIL 1948. I AM A CHARTER MEMBER OF THE OLD GUARD AND THE OLD GUARD ASSOCIATION.

COMMISSIONED 12 JANUARY 1952 BY GENERAL OMAR BRADLEY. ASSIGNED TO THE 31ST INFANTRY AND 7TH ID, KOREA JULY 1953 AND PARTICIPATED IN THE KOREAN WAR'S LAST BATTLE WHERE THE ENEMY ATTACKED OUR POSITIONS ACROSS THE CHOWAN VALLEY. AWARDED STAR FOR COMBAT INFANTRY BADGE AND 3RD BRONZE STAR FOR KOREA SERVICE. RETIRED AS A CAPTAIN JUNE 1962. AUTHOR OF "COUNTRY BOY GONE SOLDIERING."

98

CAMP ATTERBURY

Preparation for W.W.II

The Cadre from the Third Cavalry arrived at Camp Atterbury in June 1942. The barracks were new, but the grounds were a mud hole. We had to build duck boards from building to building or we would sink in mud over our shoes.

The draftees started arriving during late summer from all walks of life. Some college graduates, some high school, and a few with no formal education at all. We started a school to teach the few who could not read or write how to do so, so at least they could sign the payroll.

After we had been there a short period of time a new requirement came down that there had to be a Warrant Officer selected to be assistant communication chief. Our Regimental Communication Chief, Master Sergeant Dowd, got the job, and I was promoted from Staff Sergeant to Master Sergeant to fill Dowd's slot. Here I was, 21 years of age, with only fours years in the Army, now a Master Sergeant. I was very proud of myself, Mama and Papa were too.

About that time there was the need for a new Regimental Sergeant Major, and Newman, presently my First Sergeant, took that job. I switched jobs and took over as top kick, so my friend, Staff Sergeant Aloysius Klugiewicz, could become Master Sergeant and the Regimental Communication Chief. He was also from the Third Cavalry and I had to look out for him. To this day, he has never forgotten what I did for him. We discuss those days at our Division reunions held yearly.

My wife joined me in Indianapolis as soon as we got settled. Newman had met a lady in Indianapolis so when my wife arrived we moved in with Newman's girlfriend's family. They were a great family and very patriotic. Newman married his friend, so now we both were married. No more messing around, but we had been great lovers in our day.

It was during this period that my wife got pregnant and we made an awful mistake. We knew that I was going to war with remote possibilities of not returning, this was nuts. The odds of me not returning were very slim. However, we decided that Kitty should have an abortion, a terrible mistake. We often talked of it later and how sorry we were.

Late summer of 1942 my father died. Papa had heart disease and had a heart attack earlier. The doctor told him to do no work, not even to climb stairs. He moved his bed into a closed-in porch to comply with the doctors orders. It was very difficult for him not to perform any chores. All that he could do is sit under the apple tree by the cellar door and wave to all travelers passing by. I am sure a lot of these people stopped to say hello.

As it was late summer, the animals he still owned were in the pasture, except a large Jersey Bull that he had tied to a stake in the ground on a long chain. As the bull would graze the length of the chain all around the stake, Papa would move the stake. He was not supposed to pull, lift, or push anything strenuous, but to pull the stake proved to be his downfall. After removing the stake one day he went to his bedroom to rest. One of his grandsons, Eddie Jones, about six or seven, laid down with him, a few hours later Eddie got up and told my Mama that Grandpa wasn't breathing. When Mama went in, it was too late.

Kitty and I took the train to Washington, DC from Indianapolis; we were met at Union Station by brother Rufus. It was a sad day for me as I looked at him laid to rest in the parlor of the old house. He looked peaceful. After I viewed Papa I strolled out to the wood shed where some of Papa's old friends were standing around. They paid their respects and condolences. I had known of these men all of my life. Mr. Maurice Fox, owner of the adjoining farm was there. He being Papa's closest friend hugged me and made me very sad. After the funeral all eight of his children returned to the old home place to be with Mama for awhile. That was the only time the eight of us had ever been together.

I was twenty-one at the time, a Master Sergeant in the Army, but still a boy. After the family picture was taken I slipped off and went into a nearby cornfield and cried, staying there until I cried myself out. After my other sisters and brothers left, I am sure I spent some time close to Mama, maybe brushing her hair or sitting on the floor with my head in her lap allowing her to pat me on the face. I was still her baby boy.

George after digging potatoes.

101

Papa had planted about an acre of Irish potatoes that needed to be dug. Kitty and I hitched one horse, Beauty, to a plow and I dug the potatoes, she picking them up and placing them into bushel baskets. It was as hot as hell that day and it took us all day even with the help of Rufus's stepson, Jack Murray. After we got them all in baskets I loaded them on a drag and took them to the cellar for storage. We were dirty from the sweat and dust. As there was no bathing facilities in the house, Kitty and I went to the creek near the barn, stripped and bathed each other.

A few days later, as much as I hated to, we had to bid farewell to Mama and return to Indianapolis. Mama was not alone however, Hazel, one of my sisters lived across the road in a house that had been Papa's old General Store, now converted into a home that was located on the old mill run where the spillway was located.

After the units became full strength during the autumn months, a rigid training program began. We taught our new soldiers everything they must know. We taught them to march, run, climb, manual of arms, and military courtesy. We taught them how to dig a latrine, not a pleasant subject. In the field exercises or during actual battle, every unit had to prepare a place where one could relieve themselves. A latrine is a slit trench dug with a shovel usually four to six feet deep, depending on soil, and about one foot wide. When the ground was frozen it was not an easy chore.

To use the slit trench one would straddle it, squat, and let go. If more than one person had to go at the same time, it was an awful sight, either way, if they faced the other person or not.

I being a country boy and having seen many natural sights, this I could not stand. I tried to time it that I would be alone or go off into the brush with my individual shovel.

Upon leaving the area to move on, the trench had to be refilled with a sign posted, latrine.

As top kick I was with my company most of the time. We old soldiers from the Third Cavalry set a great example for them. We taught them how to stand, salute, make a bed, use the compass and read a map. I became a father to these men of whom most were still in their teens, yet there were some older than I, but that made no difference, I was the top kick and boss. By the time this training was over, these men were in top physical condition. Most of these young men who were just run of the mill people, except one, his name was Guess, a tall, skinny, big foot, and with a face only Mama could love. What a character. One morning at five a.m. Reveille, 1st Sergeant Newman, my close buddy called out to the formation, "Fall In", this meant to come to attention. I being a Master Sergeant stood in the rear of the company formation, when Newman yelled out, "Report," Sergeant Miller," Platoon Sergeant of the service personnel, cooks off duty, supply, driver, clerks, and the like, yelled back "1st. Platoon, one man absent," Newman listened to the other platoons report and came back to Miller and stated, "who's absent Sergeant Miller?" His reply was, "Guess." "Who," commanded the 1st Sergeant? Sergeant Miller again yelled back "Guess." With this, the 1st Sergeant had had enough of the games and stated, "Sergeant Miller," "who in the hell is absent?" Miller replied, "Private Guess, Sir." "Oh," stated the 1st. Sergeant and did an about face and reported to the company, "Commander, Sir," one man absent. Well by this time, the whole company was laughing like hell, even the Commanding Officer was laughing, I will never forget that reveille formation of years gone by.

During the training period in the fall of 1942 each company organized a touch football team, each regiment has

19 companies, so the competition was good. However, I had Fred Barnes from Philadelphia who previously had been the quarterback for the pro football team of Paterson, New Jersey. We practiced, and by being the ranking man on the team, chose to be the center, we beat everyone, won Regimental honors. Barnes would tell me, go ten and turn right, the ball was there, or he'd tell Collins to go deep, and Collins could run like a deer, the ball was there. We won Regimental and Division honors, never lost a game. Boy, were we good. However, poor Collins got hit in Normandy under a mortar barrage, evacuated never to be seen by me again. Here I go crying again.

The individual, platoon, and company training was not an easy task. The winter of 1942-1943 in Indianapolis was cold, and we trained regardless of the weather. It was so cold on one particular march, we almost froze. The next morning the Mess Sergeant could not get the cooking stove lit. Snow was also up to our butt so by noon the exercise was called off. Some of our marches were 25-30 miles with full field equipment. As top kick, I always brought up the rear, and it was rare that anyone would ever drop out.

"Short Arm" inspection was an interesting sight, everyone undressed to their underwear, I would line them up according to my roster on the clipboard and the doctor would inspect each man's penis for venereal disease and requirement of a circumcision. I would say about twenty percent needed one. This inspection was really a sight to behold, different sizes, shapes, and forms. We held this inspection monthly. I don't know where the Army thought these men would get the "Venereal Disease" as they were restricted to the base for a long period of time.

After the extremely hard winter of 1942-1943 and all of the training, our citizen soldiers had become real soldiers.

They had learned well from good instructors. We were now ready for new things to come. In June 1943, the entire Division departed Camp Atterbury to participate in an Army maneuvers in Tennessee.

After the maneuvers were over and we had won the battle, we were going to Camp Breckenridge, Kentucky. At this time, I took a ten day furlough to visit my Mama back at Waples Mill. Sergeant Klugiewicz took over the company in my absence. After everyone arrived at Camp Breckenridge, the men were given their first furlough, a few going at one time as we continued our training.

It was during these maneuvers that Newman and I almost met our fate, we had a Lieutenant who was a buddy so the three of us programmed our wives to come to Nashville for the weekend. We got rooms at a hotel and had lots of fun, in fact, too much. We got so involved that when we did leave it was late. When we arrived at the place we had left the unit, everyone had departed. We traced them and soon caught up, and were in real trouble. AWOL. The only thing that saved us was that Lieutenant Moore took all the blame. He told our Commanding Officer that Newman and I wanted to leave the hotel earlier, but that he had the only jeep. We maintained our stripes, but Lieutenant Moore was transferred out to one of the line companies as a rifle platoon leader.

My wife joined me, and I got an apartment in Evansville, Indiana, about thirty miles away. She got employment at a hotel as a desk clerk. Newman also brought his wife down from Indianapolis and shared the apartment with us.

Training continued in all phases of combat throughout the winter of 1943-1944. This winter was not as bad as the previous one.

At the completion of my furlough, Mama gave me a '39 Chevy, so when I got back to Kentucky, Newman and I had transportation to see our wives almost every night. Because of the gas shortage I had to buy gas on the black market to keep the car running. I would go by the camp bus station on the way to Evansville, pick up three or four soldiers, and charge them for the trip, this paid for the gas. On the way back to camp every morning I'd swing by the bus station in town and pick up two or three soldiers who were in line. This extra change kept us going. As a Master Sergeant in those day I made $138.00 per month.

On 6 April 1944, we were ready and loaded on a train in Kentucky headed for New York City to board the ship that had been converted to a transport ship, "The George Washington." My company being deep in the hole, we slept on triple deck canvas bunks, I did have the forethought to bring a mattress cover that I slit down one side so to have cloth under and on top of me. I remember it was crowded and a lot of men got sea sick as the ship rocked in the rough seas. At meal time, I had to hold on to my food because it would slide down the table as the ship rocked and rolled. More men got sea sick, it was the "Pits." I would take my company on deck at a specified time for exercise and fresh air. Some men could not tolerate the lower decks, so they lived on the top deck with the ocean spray, wet blankets, and the stink, etc., it was awful. We played dice and cards till the cards got wet, then we would get another deck. As the blankets and gas masks got wet they went over board. I'll bet there are tens of thousands of GI blankets and gas masks in the oceans that our military sailed on.

Two weeks later we arrived at Liverpool, England, we were met by Red Cross ladies with coffee and doughnuts, our first taste of foreign soil. We loaded our truck and moved to the Midlands. I remember that I was near a large cow pasture, pleasant spring air, flowers, and trees.

While stationed here our men were allowed passes to go into town, but had to meet bed check, I guess at that time it was 10 or 11 o'clock upon making bed check. The Charge of Quarters, usually a non-commissioned officer, reported to me that Malloy was absent, but the next morning at Reveille he had returned. I had him dig a ten foot deep by 10 foot square hole, and wrote him another pass, giving it to him with instructions to drop in the hole. I then told him to cover the pass with the dirt, he did so and after a day or so told me that I would be the first man he would shoot after reaching French soil.

We trained on all events that may occur later, recognition of foreign aircraft, how to speak "Pig" French and German, and other problems that might arise after landing in France. Being a 1st Sergeant of an Infantry company, we were not told much, we had a few radios and listened to the B.B.C. We participated in a field exercise in Wales, what a damp, dreary place in those days. After several months of this training we were delighted to hear about the invasion, we could hear the war as it was happening, we all gathered around the few radios we had. A few days later we received orders, packed up, loaded on trucks, and headed for Southampton. When we arrived at Southampton we unloaded and were told to bed down in an old warehouse. When the sun came up the next morning we dusted ourselves off from coal dust and loaded on LST's like animals. There were not toilet facilities, so we had to urinate and defecate over the side of the boat, I could "pee," but not do number two.

HEADQUARTERS 331ST INFANTRY
CAMP ATTERBURY, INDIANA

November 19, 1942.

SPECIAL ORDERS:
:
NUMBER 52 :

1. Under provisions of AR 605-115, Capt., MICHAEL E. VOIGT, O-338060, this organization, is granted leave of absence for a period of seven (7) days, effective on or about November 20, 1942.
Upon completion of leave officer will proceed to Ft. Benning, Ga. pursuant to letter GNRQU ARDIC.63-15, Subject: Orders 11-12-42.

2. Under the provisions of AR 615-5, the following named EM from organizations as indicated are promoted to grades shown, effective this date:

TO BE MASTER SERGEANT (TEMPORARY) 542 *(age 21)*
S/Sgt. George H. Waple, 6895240, Regtl Hq Co. (Existing vacancy)

TO BE STAFF SERGEANT (TEMPORARY)
T/4th Gr. Aloysius R. Klugiewicz, 6881337, Regtl Hq Co. (Existing vacancy) 539
Cpl. Harold S. Hershman, 35359008, Hq Co, 3d Bn (Existing vacancy) 821

By order of Colonel PORTER:

ROBERT C. WALKER,
1st Lt., 331st Infantry,
Adjutant.

OFFICIAL:

Robert C Walker
ROBERT C. WALKER,
1st Lt., 331st Infantry,
Adjutant.

DISTRIBUTION: "A"

Note: not many people became M Sgt @ age 21. "not bad for a country boy"

108

Our first U.S. Meeting with the Russians

Enroute to the Elbe

Waple and Newman enjoying "goodies" from home

The Buddy Group – Waple, 1st Sgt.; Mess Sgt.; Motor Sgt.

Going ashore, Normandy, June 1944

The men who served with me in WWII from Normandy to the Elbe – Some never to return – "For he who walks and sheds blood with me shall always be my brother."

EUROPE

The 83rd Infantry Division landed on Omaha Beach on D + 12 and relieved the 101 Airborne in Carenton, France. George Waple had an eventful meeting with wife, 2nd Lieutenant "Nurse" C. Waple in Frankfurt then on to the Elbe River and the conclusion of WWII.

First Sergeant George Waple resting after town was taken by the 331st

Result of kiss— twin boys.

W.W.II.

From Omaha Beach to the Elbe River

The chips were down, no turning back now, for this was the real thing, we were playing for keeps now. The weather had been against the allies since D-Day. There was a great storm, the boat rocked and rolled, no room to land, and the sea was too rough. Barrage ballons flew over each boat as bodies floated in the water. For nearly a week the waves lashed at our boats. Some were sea sick, and all were anxious to go ashore. Before our eyes lay the cliffs of France and the beaches our comrades had died on. We could hear gun shots and artillery off in a short distance, where our D-Day men were still fighting. A German plane would appear only to be blown to bits. I couldn't stand being on this hellish boat any longer. There were no facilities, and only English beans to eat. I told my company Commander, Captain Norman Whitney, that I would be awaiting for him when he came ashore. I had to go to the "John" real bad. I went over the side with only my carbine and 45 pistol. I hitched a ride on a small boat going ashore and walked up the Omaha Beach. As I walked by a hospital tent at the top of the cliff, I glanced in for a moment and kept going. I can still remember the medics and nurses tending the wounded. I walked a few hundred yards, found a tree with several other dazed GIs, and sat down. I stayed there several days, and could still hear the fighting going on inland. I was scared at night, since I'd been afraid of the dark all my life. Soon there was a voice calling for anyone belonging to the 83rd, after that, anyone in the

My men relaxing before landing at Omaha Beach

331st Infantry Regiment. I was back home with my company and kept taking roll call until all were present.

After we were again organized, we received orders to advance toward the town of Carentan and relieve a unit of the 101st Airborne Division. The rifle companies moved forward under darkness to relieve their comrades.

I set up our company command post in an old barn. The Communications Platoon was laying wire and making radio contact with subordinate units. The I&R Platoon set up an observation post and started to send out patrols. Sergeant Fred Barnes, one of the smartest men I had ever met was the I&R Platoon leader. He was a pleasure to work with and to have as a buddy. His platoon was the eyes and ears for the regiment. Several months later Barnes received a battlefield commission from Colonel Robert York our Regimental Commander. Colonel York, soon after arriving to take over our regiment, quickly recognized Barnes talents and used him as his right hand man.

By July 3rd, the Regiment was in position and thoroughly briefed on its mission. Our first attack started on July 4th, with all hell breaking loose, it was like a big Fourth of July. Artillery started at 0400 hours with two of our Battalions jumping off at 0445, both were almost stopped in their tracks. The Germans were waiting for us. There were many casualties, one being our Regimental Commander, who was in the regimental O.P. After much bitter fighting by our rifle companies against a great defensive force, our regiment was moving slowly.

I remember one instance when I was with my company Commander moving forward under the cover of darkness, we started to receive incoming mortar fire. Captain Whitney instructed us to hit the ditch. I followed him and laid face down, after awhile without further orders I fell asleep. At

Men wading ashore at Omaha Beach

day break I awoke to realize that my head was about three feet from a dead German whose body had been blown apart and I was looking at his chest cavity, an awful sight.

Once when we were moving slowly forward down a dirt "sunken" roadway with eight to ten foot banks on both sides I noticed that the Germans had dug into the banks to create bunkers. We examined each of these to make sure that no one was hiding in them. At the entrance of one I flashed my light into this large room to see an enemy soldier sitting there with his weapons across his lap. Naturally, I jumped back and called for my company Commander's interpreter, a Jewish soldier, that was with me most of the time. I asked Abe Gold to yell into the bunker and tell the German to surrender and come out. After two or three attempts to get him to come out, we moved on. It appeared that maybe he was shell shocked and would be of no harm to anyone in the future. Some soldiers from the rear probably found him later. I hope that he survived the war.

After our original Regimental Commander was killed and several more were relieved, we received a Colonel Robert York who had a lot of battle experience. The first thing he did was to move the Regimental Command Post back a few hundred yards. This brilliant Colonel remained with the Regiment throughout the war. Once I recall somewhere along the line he got wounded, sent to the hospital only to go AWOL and return to his Regiment. The reason for moving the Regimental C.P. back was because the Regimental staff found it difficult to function with flying bullets making snapping noise when passing over head cutting tree twigs that fell around the area.

I got to know Colonel York better after the war. I served with him at Fort Benning and during the Division association reunions, he retired as a Lieutenant General.

Hedgerow Country

I lost one of my men, either the first or second KIA about this time. I witnessed him drive his jeep over a mine at the entrance of the Command Post and get blown to bits. I took these KIA's very seriously, these were my soldiers. I had helped train them and was their "Top Kick." After we moved forward a few hundred yards, had gotten the regiment command post dug in and set up, my entire company was surrounded by hedge rows, we received our baptism of real fire mortar barrage. My men were trying to get cover by jumping in previous dug fox holes. When the barrage lifted, I had twenty or so men killed or wounded. After we tended to the wounded, evacuated the seriously wounded and the dead, night was setting in. I crawled in a hole and cried like a baby. It was horrible seeing those young boys getting hurt and killed that I had helped train. The next day was duty as usual. We got replacements and carried on. A day or so after the Mortar barrage, I will never forget, we had evacuated wounded and dead, I could not locate our communication platoon leader. He had run, never to return. A sick bastard in my book. Right after that, one of my section sergeants developed a sinus condition only to be evacuated and never return.

My wife had driven his car from Evansville, Indiana to New York City for storage while we were to be gone. Upon my return to the States and a few years had passed, I called this individual in New York City at his law office, I told him who I was, his old Master Sergeant, etc., his reply was, "Never heard of you." I hung up with disgust. After what we had been through back at Atterbury and Breckenridge, I guess takes all kinds.

Another outstanding soldier I lost during that mortar barrage was Collins, a good soldier who had gone deep in our football games back at Atterbury and would catch this long spiral from Barnes.

Soon we got our marching orders. The days of hell, hedgerows, and Germans were history for the moment, but never forgotten. The Germans had withdrawn to the South. As we made our way through France leaving Normandy we would pass German tanks, trucks, wagons, and animals such as cows and horses laying in the fields and beside the road way. Mostly killed during the bombing.

One of my saddest days was when I was leading some of my men across some open ground within the hedgerows. PFC Malloy of the radio section who was a feisty Irish boy was among the group. He had told me back in England that I would be the first person he would shoot when we got to France. I had given him extra duty for not making bed check and this really pissed him off. As we were moving across this pasture, one German plane flew over and dropped a bomb. We all hit the ground as the bomb exploded. When the dust cleared it was discovered that Malloy had been hit by shrapnel tearing off the end of his spine. We rushed him to the first aid tent where he was examined by our surgeon, Major Snyder. A moment later the doctor looked at me and shook his head in a negative way and stated, "it doesn't look good." Malloy was still awake and realized the wound was serious, with this he looked up at me and said, "I am sorry Sergeant Waple." We both got tears in our eyes. As tough as I tried to be inside, I was really an old softy. This young man had been trained by me and only a few years younger than I, he was like a son. He was evacuated soon, but died on the way to the field hospital. I had my second KIA, a young man who never got his day in the sun.

Our front line soldiers had captured a German Command Post, and with the group was a 1st. Sergeant just as I. I had learned to tell the rank of the enemy and immediately could see that we had a 1st Sergeant. I walked up to him and introduced myself and asked if he spoke English. His reply was in English so we immediately became, even though enemies, friends. He was dressed smartly in his shinny boots, breeches, and blouse. A smart looking soldier. He also had in his hands a pair of black leather gloves, the type of mittens with a trigger finger. I admired the gloves and asked for them. His reply was that his mother had given them to him and would like to keep them. I could never argue with this answer. He was finally called for interrogation by our intelligence people and I went on my way. In a while, one of my men came and found me to tell me that the German 1st. Sergeant would like to see me. I was nearby and was there in seconds. Upon walking up to him he handed me the gloves stating that he realized that he would have to surrender them somewhere up the line and wished for me to have them. I was gracious, shook his hand and he was led away. The war was over for him. He probably came to the states and worked on a farm as a trusted prisoner of war.

Having access to the Regimental Command Post, I could follow the war from the maps displayed at all times. From July 4th throughout the month our front line troops fought hard. With the Germans fighting a defensive war, knowing the terrain was to their benefit. They continually counter attacked. My friend Barnes tells the story, I've heard it a hundred times, that once one of his superiors told him to go and find a position for a future Command Post. This Colonel pointed to a "Goose Egg" on the map. Barnes reply to him was, "did you get permission from the German General for me to go there." Barnes knew his business, knew more about

where the enemy was than most. That is why Colonel York depended on him so much.

We advanced slowly, taking many casualties, my friend Marcel, the Sergeant Major, got the morning reports from the line companies through their respective Battalion reflecting losses, replacements would arrive, be sent for by a Battalion runner and assigned as needed. Some of these soldiers looked lost, eyes scared. They would report to a line company at late afternoon or evening, some to never see the sun rise again. They would report to a squad, meet the Corporal, and the Company would attack at five AM, some would be dead by six AM, some never fired a shot.

July 25th was a day I'll never forget. I heard the roar of planes, the sky was full of planes, and reports stated there were 2,500 of them. Bombs began to fall over the German lines, fighters were overhead, a beautiful sight as the bombs fell, my trousers shook from the earth vibrating. As the bombs fell dust began to rise, and bombs began to fall shorter and shorter, some on our own troops waiting to attack.

The Normandy Campaign was drawing to a close. Our Regiment had been fighting for 23 continuous days. There was a short break, we got fresh clothing and socks, we had been in these clothes for a month or so. I got undressed for a much needed shower and discovered that I had lice or crabs, showered everything, used blue ointment.

From Normandy we proceeded into the Brittany Campaign. The memory I have here is when our Regiment fought at St. Malo after clearing the town, there was a large hill called the Citadel, it extended into the bay. The Germans would not give up. Our forces sent artillery, bombers, fighters with bombs, some going into the entrance of the hill, finally our troops took the objective. One hill that I went through had many tunnels and off the main tunnel were rooms that the Germans operated from. Some dead Germans still sat at their tables or at their desk, it was some sight. This is where I found my lugar pistol that I kept throughout the war, but was stolen years later.

After St. Malo, there were more hedgerows, but the fighting was not as intense. Many Germans were captured during this campaign, our Regiment capturing some 4,000.

At the end of the Brittany Campaign our Regiment ended up near a town of Nantes, at the Loire River. We received many replacements, and while still in contact with the Germans there was time to rest. We were allowed to go to town and it wasn't long before my men found the French ladies very friendly. I guess we were taking over from the Germans of last week. Marcel, my buddy, friends, comrades and I were strolling through the city one evening, sightseeing, when we heard American music coming from inside a building with a sign over the front door stating "American Bar." Probably several weeks ago it was called, The "German Bar." I knocked on the door and low and behold the most beautiful lady, that I had seen in a long time, opened the door. We were invited in and what do you know, the owner of the bar was even more attractive than the one that had opened the door. This lady owned the bar, her name "Pomme," means apple in English. In stock she had Johnny Walker Scotch and Segrams VO, not bad for a bombed out French town. Marcel and I had drinks and danced. Upon closing time we walked the ladies home, "Pomme," being at my side, was very apologetic about her residence, but I insisted that I see her home. Upon arriving at her place I was amazed, it was an apartment house with an iron grill all around. On entering the front door there was a lobby with beautiful furniture, and she escorted me to her suite just off the lobby. During the week or so rest period I saw her every evening, and I was sad to leave Nantes. I wrote her several times during the war with hopes of returning someday, but she soon faded away from my thoughts.

I spoke of Sergeant Fred Barnes early, about him getting a battlefield commission, with this he got a clothing allowance that officers got in those days for dress uniform and accessories. He needed that money for clothing like I needed a hole in the head. We got permission of our Commanding Officer and spent several days sight seeing Nantes and visiting with the ladies of the evening. We still discuss those beautiful sights of Nantes, France at our reunions. In Nantes my men located a brothel that almost at anytime I could hold reveille there. One evening when about one third of my company was at this residence, the Regimental Executive Officer, strolled in with his driver. A buck Sergeant, who was the motor pool Sergeant, was fond of the most attractive lady in the establishment. She also liked Sgt. Hare, an old country boy from Pee Dee, SC, and as I recall, I can't remember why, recalling the short arm inspection of the past. Well, the Executive Officer wanted to meet Hare's friend, but both the lady and Hare were reluctant to yield. I stepped in so there would be no trouble and convinced Sergeant Hare that it would be in the best interest for all if he let his friend visit with the Colonel, if not, he may put the house off limits. Everyone lived happily from then on. The madam and I became close friends in that short period and upon leaving she gave me a nice bonus for our patronage. After Normandy and Brittany this had been great fun.

After checking my initial roster of the landing force of my company, I found that I had lost some thirty men or so through wounds, killed or unfit for duty.

Before leaving Brittany word spread that one of our sister regiments had captured 25,000 Germans. I remember going by a compound where they were being detained. They had been told to take everything from their pockets, paper money and German marks covered the ground. Some of us picked several notes up for souvenirs only to find out later that this type of money was still being used in Luxembourg our next stop.

After being relieved by another unit our Regiment motored across France arriving in late September in Luxembourg. The Regimental Command Post was in a large hotel in the town of Senningen, on the outskirts of the City of Luxembourg. This was a beautiful place. All of the officers slept in the hotel with my men and me in the out buildings. This is where I decided that if I ever fought in another war, I wanted to be an officer.

This was good living, compared to Normandy. We could get passes to the city and somewhere I met another attractive lady, the daughter of a banker, as I recall, we became friendly. She invited me to meet her parents and for dinner, good living. It was at this area where Marcel received notice from his wife that he was the father of a baby boy. He and I went to town and tied one on. When we came back to our Command Post, we got into the same bedding roll, he got sick and puked all over us, what a mess. It was also the same location where Lieutenant Fred Barnes, now being a 2nd Lieutenant living with the officers on the 2nd floor of the chateau, had too much to drink one evening. When he went to bed he laid the opposite way he usually slept. Upon awaking later and having to go to the toilet, he instead of walking out the room through the door, walked out of the full length window, fell about 15-20 feet to the ground, but was not injured. The guard on the front door thought we were being raided by airborne troops.

With all of Luxembourg liberated, and as I recall, with no orders to go further than the Moselle River, we started training again and had passes to town. Thanksgiving of 1944 was in Luxembourg. I had dinner with a girl that I had met and her family. They were wonderful people. I remember at the end of November we were to advance across the river with a larger force, but the plans were changed, so we sat again for a few days guarding Luxembourg. Our next move was to head for the Hurtgen Forest, East of Aachen, where we were to relieve the 4th Infantry Division. As I rode with my company Commander into this forest, where I could see many had to have died, it was a thicket, much like General Jackson encountered in the Civil War battle called the "Wilderness," near Chancellorsville, Virginia. The pine tree tops had been blown off and fell to engulf the already undergrowth. There were ruts in the dirt road that were almost impassable, but the ground was frozen. I remember seeing arms and legs of soldiers, some German and some of ours sticking out of the frozen mud by the side of the road. The graves registration units would come by, dig the body out, or if it was to mangled, cut the part that was intact off an edge of frozen earth. Boy, it was cold. When we arrived at our "goose egg" on the map, I set up the command post. I had been a pretty good wood chopper as a boy so we built a log hut for the Colonel and his staff. I inherited a nice fox hole dug by a German, I guess. It was about three feet deep, covered with logs, tree branches from a pine tree, and more dirt. Sergeant Miller, my supply Sergeant, and I shared it for a few days. On the 24th of December, we were being relieved to head for the Battle of the Bulge. I remember having Christmas dinner in an old building in Aachen, I had

We crossed the Siegfried line east of Eupen…the dragon's teeth of this formidable defense now seemed like mere miniature monuments.

We moved through Aachen and to the edges of the Hurtgen Forest where we detrucked and started our march into the forest to relieve the battered men of the 4th Division.

Heavy artillery from the woods pounded around us…we sought momentary cover…and then we were up again and attacking across the open plain into the forest.

And by the time we reached the edges of the Forest, our linemen were repairing wires and a call sent in – mission accomplished... armored units were now able to advance and cut the vital Houffalize-St. Vith highway...

The best the Nazis could hurl at us was destroyed.

We dug in and got our guns and bayonets ready for the offensive…and by the second night we dug deeper and covered our foxholes with logs for it took only one night to realize the deadly effect of tree bursts coming from Nazi heavy artillery.

These log-covered holes became our shelters and living quarters for almost a month…Nazi propaganda leaflets actually tried to frighten us with such warnings as "death lurks behind every tree" but we just read them with scorn and ridicule.

Our battalion CPs and the Regimental CP were built into the earth, log-cabin style to give room for the staffs and a little protection from shells.

In the rear echelons of our Combat Team, we built fires near the kitchens and warmed our chilled bodies when we had the chance...Broken tree-tops were mute testimony of the blanket shelling the Nazis laid upon us.

The mortarmen…and our scouts ever at the front, drawing enemy fire, enemy shells.

The Belgium bulge was shrinking…we pursued the enemy farther into the forest…we were tired…we were cold…our physical stamina was sapped.

We were cautious in our approach but our advance was steady.

Up high ground, in the face of enemy small arms, mortar and artillery fire, we fought and punched our way forward…

Digging the Nazis from their ever-winding entrenched positions in the hills.

Our units in Bihain repulsed a vicious counterattack and the town was soon blazing from burning Nazi tanks and houses.

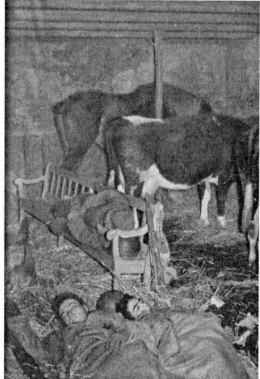

Our only chance for rest was in barns where we sought the warmth of hay.

139

Across snow-covered open ground, we attacked…in every house, every barn, lurked Nazis.

The doughboy – tired, bearded and unkempt – was again triumphant.

Kitchens, too, had to improvise if we were to be fed any hot meals…a few cooks converted captured German trucks into mobile kitchens and if we stopped for as long as three or four hours in one place, a hot meal awaited us.

"K" rations, the worse ration ever, a small can of spam, chocolate bar, and crackers. We had just been fighting the Germans for the first time on German soil.

As we moved toward the Battle of the Bulge snow covered the ground, it was cold. I was riding in the back seat of the company Commander's jeep. It was dark and we moved slowly, no lights. Then all of a sudden I felt the jeep go off the road into a ditch, being on its side I was tossed into the deep snow. I had on everything I could get on and laying there in the snow I felt warm. I said to myself, Oh Lord, just let me stay here for the rest of the war. With the jeep now upright, we moved on into the Battle of the Bulge. Where I was, where the enemy was, no one knew most of the time. I remember setting up our company Command Post in a barn with cows present, the warmth from their bodies helped keep the barn warm. The unit we relieved at the Bulge had taken a real beating, bodies of our troops were stacked head to toe, like a cord of wood, an awful sight. After we got settled in, some mail caught up to us. I received a package from my sister, a cake, and when I sliced into it there was a pint of whisky. Fred (Lieutenant) Barnes and I drank it in two swallows and got back to business.

As we were advancing across Europe we experienced the buzz bombs heading for England. Further along as we approached Germany, I witnessed a beautiful sight of our Air Force P-38 dogfight with German planes it was like a circus. It was wonderful to watch our Air Force B-17s fly over knowing they were heading for the manufacturing areas in Germany. Once when they were returning, one B-17 was on fire, we watched as it pulled out of the formation, one by one the crew bailed out. Then there was a pause, another body bailed out, and the plane flew on for a few seconds and exploded. I guess the last body was the pilot, brave comrades. One parachute landed not to far from our position.

As we advanced toward the Germans in The Bulge my regiment was attached to the 3rd Armored Division for Infantry Support. As we reached an all important highway that went from St. Vith-Houffalize, we met General Patton coming from the South. In a famous picture there he stood in the turret of a tank directing traffic. I have often wondered what would have happened had he realized that there goes First Sergeant Waple, who had only a year ago been my Horse Orderly— he probably would have said, "Give 'em hell, Sergeant!"

The 83rd was relieved, and we moved back for a short rest. No enemy in sight since June back near Carentan. I remember that we cleaned up, got fresh clothing, boots, cleaned weapons, and got ready to move on.

The fighting through the Rhineland was more a gentlemen's war from my perspective. From the Command Post I could follow the fighting on the map, where the other regiments were, and who was doing what. The rivers and cities were being defended by the Germans. I remember the open fields where farms had been. During one advance we received rifle fire from a barn several hundred yards away. We jumped into a ditch with one of my soldiers, in front of me. My head at his feet as we crawled toward the barn. Suddenly he stopped moving. I yelled, "Keep moving," no response, so I crawled up beside him and when my eyes got even with his I could see where a bullet had gone into his forehead, another of my boys dead.

We were moving pretty swiftly now through Central Europe. Spring weather had been good, in fact, great, after the Hurtgen Forest and Battle of The Bulge, summer was coming.

On our way East, at one point, we were moved to Holland, I set up my Command Post in a nice residential home where a man, wife, and daughter lived. The young lady had a boyfriend who took me aside after a few days and asked me if I had any condoms. Me, what would I be doing with condoms, however, I was able to find some for him.

We were really rolling now, set up a Command Post, tear it down, move, we were rolling toward the Eble River. Everyone wanted to get there first to meet the Russians. We had picked up so much German equipment and vehicles, that we looked like a circus troop. I had my kitchen set up in a large trailer that we had found, it was great, dry, stoves level, and the like. We were told to get rid of it soon, however, by Higher Headquarters when we got to the Elbe. A bridge had been built across the river called the Truman Bridge, at Barby. On April 13, elements crossed the river, exact date that I crossed, I don't recall, I remember setting up our company Command Post in a cellar full of potatoes, safe but bumpy to sleep on. Soon we met the Russians. The war was over in May, and we were about sixty miles from Berlin. Here I was 60 miles from Berlin, and I knew we would pull back. I'd been to England, no London, France, no Paris, and now no Berlin.

We moved back a short distance and then onto Bavaria for the occupation of Germany. I saw Austria, the Danube River, and some beautiful country. I took a bus ride to the Berchtesgaden, Hitler's retreat. It had been blown apart. I have pictures of us there, Captain Whitney, my CO, M/Sergeant Klugiewicz, and Lieutenant Thornton, it was so peaceful.

We got new GI uniforms, the wool shirt, trousers, and Ike jacket. I was trim and looked "spiffy." Where my regiment settled there had been a Hungarian horse unit, me being an old trooper of the 3rd US Cavalry enjoyed the riding and jumping. The Commanding Officer of the Cavalry unit had a gorgeous blonde friend, she also became my friend. We went on several jeep rides, sat and talked in a pine forest on pine needles, she was lovely.

Late summer we started rotating home. There was a point system being used, men with families and Purple Hearts left first. My turn came as did my old buddies M/Sergeant "Kelly," Klugiewicz, and Marcel, the Sergeant Major, and my close friend from August 1938, when we joined the 3rd Cavalry at Ft. Myer, Virginia. We had been together seven years-like Siamese twins. In the 3rd Cavalry, to M/Sergeant's, and a World War under our belts; he left before I as he had one child and five more points. I never served with him again.

After my friend Marcel rotated home he attended Officer Candidate School at Fort Riley, Kansas. He stayed for twenty years and retired as a Major in the DC area to become Chief of Security at Walter Reed Hospital, Silver Springs, Maryland. We never saw much of each other. He had his thing and I guess I had mine. He passed on in the late eighties, and as I was in the hospital at the time could not attend his funeral at Arlington. He received full honors as I hope I will someday.

After leaving my company, I was sent to an assembly point where other high point men were gathering from other units. I was made First Sergeant in a unit of the 99th Infantry Division. There I had been with the 83rd from 1942 throughout the war. Now I was being sent home under colors of another Division, one that had seen very little action. After filling the unit we railed to Marseille, France, for deportation to the good ol' USA.

Before we shipped out for Marseille, the entire Division was trucked to a large field where General Patton was to bid us farewell. He stood on a large platform in his beautiful uniform and pearl handle pistols and told us in no uncertain terms we had won the war. He looked like a giant of a man that I remembered back at Fort Myer in 1938–1940. Being located in a position to where I could easily get to the platform, I asked Mast Sgt. Klugiewicz to take charge of the company. At this time with General Patton still giving his farewell speech, I moseyed down to the platform. Seeking out his aide standing nearby I introduced myself and told him of my past history with the General when I was his orderly at Fort Myer in 1939. He absorbed my story and when the General dismounted from the platform, the aide pulled him aside and talked to him briefly. With this, the General turned and greeted me like a long lost brother. "Waple," he said, "I see we both got promoted during the war." He hugged me and congratulated me on the great job the 83rd Division had done. "Sure, I remember you. You were the best goddamn orderly I ever had." With this, he bid me good luck while shaking my hand as he got into his staff car, saying, "When you get back to the States, you let those bastards who won this war." Again, I, too, felt like a giant as other surrounding members of his staff looked on.

We lay around Marseille for a week or ten days, as I recall, and went into the city several times, it was nice. At our company, we were housed in tents, no electricity, but had several Coleman lanterns. Sergeant Miller, who had been with me as my Supply Sergeant for the entire war, and I, built a dice table from scraps of wood, side boards, and all. We had the only lantern and ran a cut crap game, we cut (ace-duce); made a few hundred dollars each. We had been paid up to date, in ten dollar denomination bills, so one had to shoot at least ten dollars. Had we not shipped out we would eventually had all the money, that is from anyone who wanted to shoot craps. Before we loaded aboard the ship to come home, there was an order that all foreign pistols were to be turned in. I bought them all, at least all I could carry. As First Sergeant, I had a field desk which I filled with all the pistols I bought, about 29 of them. It took two men to carry the desk on and off the boat. Later on, after I got assigned to Fort Myer, my original station, I gambled some and I wasn't the sharpest poker player. As I ran low on cash I would put up a pistol or two. Finally, I had lost them all, except one Luger and P-38, both of these were later stolen. So, easy come, easy go. On the ship returning home everyone was gambling, I was lucky and won over $1,000.00

I remember, my ol' buddy, Kelly, had to borrow from me as he lost. When we arrived back in the States, he went his way and I went mine, however, he owed me over $500.00 and promised to pay me when he got settled. I thought this would never happen, but he paid every cent $50, $100, at a time. At this writing, we are still good W.W.II pals and see each other every year at the reunions. After I left for overseas, my wife Kitty, who was a nurse, joined the Army, took her basic training at Atlantic City and then overseas to Europe. After the war and we had pulled back, I got permission to visit her. She being a Lieutenant and me First Sergeant created some problems. Her Commanding Officer, a Major, forbid us to see each other alone. I went to the 1st Sergeant of the medical company and told him my story, his reply was sneak into my room, here is the key. I will sleep elsewhere for a few days. That favor was from one 1st Sergeant to another.

While I am on the subject of my first wife, I may as well tell about another incident of visiting her. After we moved to

Bavaria, I got permission again to visit her. She was now near Reims, France. Upon arriving she was told by her Commanding Officer that I could not see her alone again. So we took a ride in my jeep that my Commanding Officer had let me take. We ended up with one extra jeep, one that was not on the books. The ride was into the City of Reims. In driving around I saw a sign on a building stating "Officers Club" I stopped, we went inside and met with the duty officer. I told him our story, and he said use my room. I really don't believe he felt that this Lieutenant Nurse was my wife, but probably felt, Oh Well, more power to the Sergeant, if he can pick up a Lieutenant Nurse. The result of this evening's activities as twin boys born March 9, 1946. When Kitty realized that she may be pregnant, she went for a rabbit test which confirmed she was. Upon reporting this to her unit she was sent back to the States, even arriving before me. The babies were born about 30 - 40 days ahead of time and when I use to tell people that I got back to the States in Nov. 1945, and that the babies were born in March, they usually would count the month span, figuring how could this happen, George got home in November and the twins were born in March. I would not tell them right away that Kitty had been to Europe and the babies were conceived in July 1945.

On my arrival back to the States, I had orders to report to Ft. Meade, MD for discharge. I had landed in Boston so took the train to Fort Meade, Maryland. After reporting in I was told to return the next day for processing. I hitched a ride from Ft. Meade to the border of Washington, DC, I was in uniform and when I hailed a cab for transportation to Alexandria, Virginia, where my wife and mother were visiting with my sister Frances, the cabby stated, "Sergeant from here to Alexandria will cost you ten dollars." He did not know that I had about $1,000 in a binocular case with the strap around my neck. I stated "OK," I got ya covered. When we arrived at my sister's, I opened the binocular case, pulled out my roll of all tens, and peeled out a single ten, gave it to him with no tip, his eyes almost "popped" out. Upon entering the house, I greeted my Mama, put the money in her lap, kissed my sister and grabbed my wife, if she was not already pregnant, she soon would be.

I got processed and discharged the next day. Now a civilian for the first time since August 1938, I had no plans so laid around for ten days. Missing the Army, on Nov. 24, 1946, I reenlisted getting myself reassigned to Ft. Myer, Virginia, my original Army home as First Sergeant of the Ceremonial Detachment. This unit handled all burials at Arlington, the Tomb Guard, Honor Guards for visiting dignitaries to Washington DC, and the like. I was back in heaven.

I have walked up the road cut into the cliff at Normandy, settled in at Carentan, walked through the Hedgerows, witnessed some sorry moments, had a few laughs, rode across France, saw what reminded me of Jackson at the Wilderness near Chancellorsville, Virginia, in the Hurtgen forest, almost froze during the Battle of the Bulge, observed some sights in crossing Europe that were a sight to behold, soldiered with some of the bravest men ever to serve their Country, and was proud to be a part of it. Just go, fight, dig in, get up, move out, and some to die. Why did some die? They died doing their job for our Great Country. Yes, we bitched, yet we fought because we thought it was the thing to do. I am so proud to have been a part of it. Also, when I look at the original picture of the men I went into Normandy with hanging in my den, I salute them every day. I only wish I could gather all of the ones that remain alive today and toss the dice against a footlocker.

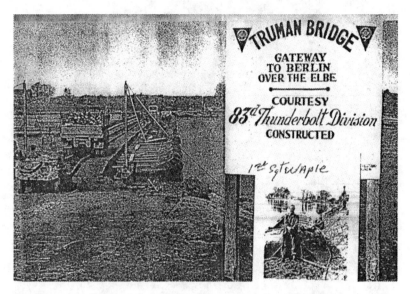

The Truman Bridge was built as we clung to our positions on the bridgehead, and a hundred yards to the south the Franklin Memorial pontoon bridge was constructed to maintain a constant flow of traffic east and west then began the alert job of guarding these bridges against floating mines and Nazi suicide swimmers.

The 331st Infantry of the 83rd Infantry Division may not be known as well as men of the 4th, 29th, and 1st Infantry Divisions, but we put on our boots the same way as they did. We ate the same German bullets that they ate, but I do want to say thanks to each and every one of those men who fought in those Divisions, they were brave bastards the way they stormed those beaches. Every time I see those films I cannot help but to cry. God bless them all.

First Sgt. Waple, wreath bearer for Pres. Truman, 1946.
Note Waple holding President Truman Hat.
Memorial Day, 1946

The Military District, Washington D.C.

As First Sergeant of the Ceremonial Detachment from 1945 to 1948, George Waple functioned as usher at the White House for Affairs of State and was often in the presence of the President and Cabinet Members. He was the coach and manager of the Ft. Myer baseball team.

THE WHITE HOUSE
WASHINGTON

12 March 1947

Dear Captain Calvert:

The Presidential Receptions for the winter season,
1946-1947, have now been concluded and the following
men are hereby released from duty on this assignment.

1st Sergeant George H. Waple
Master Sergeant Alvin F. Meyer, Jr.
Staff Sergeant Henry S. Pickerel
Staff Sergeant James W. Wilmer
Staff Sergeant Clay V. Wood
Staff Sergeant Earl W. Smith Sr.
Staff Sergeant Wilfred Smith
Sergeant Floyd L. McGee
Sergeant Clifford M. Hestdalen
Corporal Harold L. Adkins

It is not anticipated that men will be needed for
this duty until next fall, but I do wish at this time
to commend these men on the fine job they did during
the past season here at the White House.

Sincerely

/s/ H H Vaughan
/t/ HARRY H. VAUGHAN
Major General, U. S. Army
Military Aide to the President

A TRUE COPY:

GEORGE H WAPLE
2d Lt   INF

153

POST W.W.II

Ft. Myer, VIRGINIA

I left home a boy, grew up some in the next few years, and got to talk with my father only once as a man. I wished he had lived longer so that we could have become friends, and that he could have seen his post W.W.II son, and father of twin boys. He loved children and I am sure he would have gone nuts over the boys. I could have told him about the war, about the people, and their life style. Here I am back at Fort Myer, in an important assignment with no Papa to share my experiences with.

Upon reporting to my new assignment I could not get housing on Fort Myer right away. I was lucky that my sister Fran had a friend who was getting a divorce and had an apartment full of furniture. The lady arranged it with the rental agent for me to get the apartment as I was buying all of the furniture. We moved in and set up housekeeping, it was about three miles from Ft. Myer.

My mother had bought one of the last cars in 1942, a Pontiac, which she sold to me so I had transportation. It was only a few months when I was notified that quarters were available on the Fort. They were sub standard, with a coal stove for heat and the old time radiators. It was very dirty and the radiators made noises when they heated up, real dusty too. We managed, and were told that as I was a 1st Sergeant I would get the next set of quarters available. This quarters would be a very nice two story brick building, and great for the twins born on March 9, 1946. Before we moved, I was living next door to a Sergeant Dry, who was General

Eisenhower's chauffeur. In the spring of 1948, Sergeant Dry would take the twins over to General and Mrs. Eisenhower who would be out back of Quarters #1 working in their flower garden. General Ike was the Chief of Staff of the Army at this time. When General Eisenhower retired, the twins were now walking and their mother had them near by on the lawn of the temporary quarters that General and Mrs. Eisenhower were living.

I was in charge of the Honor Guard standing in the street in front of the quarters. General Eisenhower had moved out of Quarters #1 so the new Chief of Staff could move in, who was General Bradley. As General Eisenhower came out of the house, he noticed my twins standing on the grass near by, he asked his aide to get two of his books which he autographed and gave to the boys, I was very proud of this.

Speaking of the twins, as stated, they were born on March 9, 1946. Prior to the week of March 9, my wife did not feel good so my oldest sister Hazel came to stay with us. March 9th was a Saturday, my wife's water broke on the night of the 8th, and my sister and I rushed her to Arlington, Virginia, hospital. Hazel stayed with her, and I went home as we were having the usual Saturday morning full dress inspection. After I had formed the company for inspection, the Charge of Quarters yelled from the porch of the barracks, "Sergeant Waple, your wife had twins" the entire company applauded. M/Sergeant Myers took over the company and I was granted permission to leave. The twins were premature about a month or so and weighed only 3 1/2 & 4 lbs., ugly as rats. Their heads about the size of a tennis ball. They had to remain in an incubator for 30 days. At that size my wife Kitty, had only to grunt and they popped out. We prepared their cribs and rooms real nice, as we had a month to do so. When we did bring them home they needed to be fed every

155

two hours, what a pain for six months or so, the 10-12-2 & 4 feeding was rough. I would fall asleep and the bottle would slip out of the mouth of the one I was feeding, causing him to cry and waking me up. It was tough sleeping for quite awhile as I would leave the house 6 am, not returning until about 5:30 PM. We were up most of the night and all day.

I also had to keep the coal stove going all night too, the house was old and not insulated very good, but we made it. The next spring came and we were on our way. Moving later that summer to bigger and better housing. Our new home was a three bedroom duplex with a basement. Although we still heated with coal, the furnace was there. It was in this basement that I first taught the twins to play ball. Very soon after we moved in my oldest brother Ralph got a position with the Post Engineer Department and was in charge of all interior painting. He would stop by the house and have coffee with Kitty and see the twins. It wasn't too long before my new home was painted with any color Kitty wished. We had the prettiest home on the block. As Ralph left home early and I came late, I never got to know this brother like the rest.

After W.W.II when I was stationed at Fort Myer, the Assistant Division Commander during the war, General Ferenbaugh, and about twenty other 83rd men organized a Division Association at Fort Myer. I am one of a few living that were charter members.

I was never active in the Association after my Fort Myer tour until I fully retired in 1985. Since then, Violet, my second wife, and I have attended every one. They are held in various cities around the country. I enjoy seeing my old buddies very much, the war stories get better every year. There are two from my Company that show up every year, Fred Barnes, my main man, who got a direct commission in

Normandy, and Alex Klugiewicz who had gone from the Third Cavalry with me to the Infantry, and W.W.II.

WWII members 831D Chartening Association of the 83rd Infantry Division, including General Ferenbaugh (center) 1st Sgt. Waple (second from left), and Lt. Newman, (far left). Fort Myer, Va., 1946

There is also a New Jersey Chapter of about twenty-five. We have a Christmas party every year and reminisce about the good old days. I find that the only thing really good about the good old days was that I was younger. Like in golf, the older I get the better I use to play.

At the Division reunion we conduct a memorial service honoring our former buddies. It is nice, but sad, someone will read the names of our comrades who have passed on since last year, followed by a song by one of our friends, called "My Buddy." There is not a dry eye in the ballroom.

There is a banquet with good music and I am always amazed that none of us have forgotten to "jitterbug."

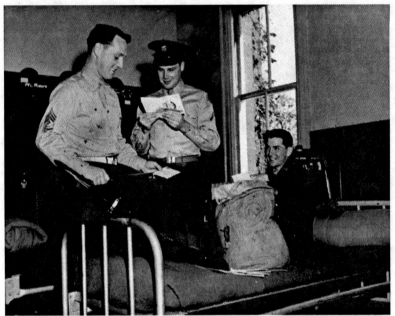

Sgt. George Waple and two of his soldiers pictured in Ft. Myer, Va, 1946, reading mail received as a result of a radio show announcement about Soldier walking guard at tomb of unknown soldier.

I did not realize at the time when I became first Sergeant of the Unit, called the Ceremonial Detachment, in November of 1945, that later I would become the First Sergeant of "A" Company, Third Infantry Regiment "The Old Guard", The President's Own. The Third Infantry Regiment was reactivated on 5 April 1948. It was a delight to be in this position and later in my story you will read that, in retirement, I became a Distinguished Member of the Old

Guard Association. I just happened to be the oldest member of that Association, age and time wise.

I was busy being 1st Sgt. of the Ceremonial Detachment. We were probably the sharpest unit in the US Army at that time, complete spit and polish at all times At the most important ceremonies I would put myself in charge so as to get in the lime light. I was wreath bearer for high ranking dignitaries who would place a wreath at the Tomb of Unknown Soldier, the highest ranking person being President Truman. I did it for him on several occasions, as can be proved by pictures I have holding his hat while he laid the wreath. One time he asked me if I knew the bugler who blew taps, I said, "Yes, sir." With that he told me to tell him that he did one hell of a job.

During the winter of 1946 and 1947, the White House had requested that my unit provide ten soldiers to act as junior aides for the winter reception season, naturally, I put myself in charge. I selected nine other of my best and reported for duty when they called. We would receive the guest at the front door and direct them where to go. We lined them up four abreast preceding the receiving line of the President, the Guest of Honor, and his wife. After all guests arrived we were allowed to mingle, have a cocktail, and eat. After the last winter reception and President Truman got used to seeing us around, he asked me if I thought my soldiers would like to remain after all guests had left to have a cocktail or two, and that he would play the piano and we would sing. As the President had been a Captain in W.W.I, an artillery man, we had to sing "As the Caissons Go Rolling Along." Some time after sipping artillery punch, singing and eating, President Truman directed the Secret Service to escort us back to Ft. Myer, an evening to remember.

Getting settled in my new assignment as First Sergeant, of probably the sharpest unit in the Army at that time, was very satisfying to me. I learned the operation quickly, I was involved in writing a new drill and ceremonial manual, and to make the unit even better looking. DA approved that my unit be issued the tropical worsted uniforms for ceremonies, the same uniform as the officers wore for summer, we were sharp. I have a picture of me modeling the uniform with my company Commander, Capt. Ross Calvert.

I had access to receiving the best looking soldiers that arrived in the area, all about 5-10 to 6-2. I would recruit them from Ft. Meade and Ft. Belvoir. The unit also housed the men who walked at the Tomb of the Unknown Soldier, had the horses and caisson for bodies deserving the privilege. I was in high cotton as top kick of this unit. One of our visitors at the Tomb was Don McNeil of the radio show, Chicago. Upon his return to work he told of our unit over the radio and the job we were doing. We received mail bags full of letters from all over the Country. The unit also had good athletic teams. I was on the champion bowling team.

As my unit dropped in strength due to regular discharge, I would request to our personnel department that I needed twenty or so outstanding soldiers who would have at least two years left on their enlistment. The S-1 of Fort Myers would call other installations in the area telling them what type of soldier I needed. Those requests were usually filled without question except for one time. One day two truck loads of soldiers arrived. I left the orderly room to go greet my new men and to look them over. All went well until the last couple of men jumped down from the truck.

Now for the story about Rebock.

I greeting him cordially and asked what he was doing there. "I don't know, Sarge, but my other First Sergeant told me this morning to get my gear and get on that truck, so here I am." What a sight, all of the other men had gone off to a formation, but nearly, they were giggling their heads off. I told Rebock to follow me to my orderly room. He had to bend to get into the door. He stood about six feet six, foot size had to be a fifteen and ugly. I called the personnel office reporting that I had received a truckload of replacements from Fort Belvoir and told him about Rebock.

He told me to hold on, that he would call their personnel office right away and get back to me. With this, I escorted Rebock to the day room, told him to take his pack off and rest. Soon the personnel office got back to me and said, "Sgt. Waple, you're stuck with him." At first, I was pissed off, then I interviewed Rebock and found he was a really nice man, but ugly as hell. I assigned him his quarters and told him where the mess hall was and to report to me tomorrow morning. The next day, at six a.m., he reported, long legs, arms down to his knees, Adam's apple protruding, still ugly.

I took him to the boiler room, as in those days we still burned coal, and instructed him that he was to be the permanent fireman, not an attractive job. He reply was, "Yes, sir, First Sergeant." Well, in a day or two, I visited the boiler room to find the place spic and span. Not dust, no loose coal lying around and a room nearby that had been filled with junk cleared and several chairs, a table and magazines for his pleasure set up. The place was beautiful.

After several months of this, Rebock came to my office saying he didn't want to be a fireman; the coal dust affected his cough. I said, "Okay, I'll make you a latrine orderly. I told him what his job was, and immediately the latrine was perfect and when I would inspect about nine-thirty or so, Rebock would greet me: "Latrine ready for inspection." With this, all stool lids would pop up. Everything was perfect, no paper, no soap out of place, no stains, floor shining. Rebock was doing a hell of a job, except one day, he came to my office and said he did not want to be a latrine orderly. "Okay. What do you want?" I asked him. "I want to be a cook," Rebock replied.

I buzzed the Mess Sergeant, telling him Rebock wanted to be a cook, he said that was fine, knowing that both he and I realized what Rebock would actually be doing in the kitchen: permanent kitchen police. The Mess Sgt. took Rebock to the kitchen.

In about a month, Rebock came to my office again, this time, pissed off. he said, "Look, Sergeant, I've done everything you have asked of me: fireman, latrine orderly, kitchen police... Now I want to be a cook." Again, I buzzed the Mess Sergeant and told him to make Rebock a third cook (there was no third cook). Rebock got behind the serving table, helped service meals, got pots and pans for the cooks and observed the Army cooking style. It wasn't long before a second cook job was open and Rebock was given the job. Now to make a long story short, Rebock went on to become first cook, sent to cook's and baker's school. In a few years, he became Mess Sergeant, married a nurse, and lived happily ever after. He retired from the Army. The last I heard from him was that he was head chef in a Washington hotel.

At baseball, I was pretty good – could cover all positions. We had a great championship softball team, as well as baseball. Most of this talent came from the fact that we had the pick of the crop of men.

Our team would play other military teams surrounding the Washington area. I believe it was in 1947 that a Captain Oppenheimer who was in Special Service at the Pentagon contacted me with reference to forming a military District of Washington baseball team. We took the best players from around the area and fielded a good team. We then started to play better teams from Fort Meade, Fort Lee, the Navy or any other military teams that would play us. I normally played second base and was a pretty fair hitter.

Later on, when the Korean War news broke and the draft started again, Captain Oppenheimer was in a position to pick some major leaguers that were assigned to Fort Myer. John Antonelli, Calderone, Purkey, and others, some AAA, some AA players were picked. It was not long before I became out classed and turned in my suit. When John Antonelli reported to the Fort, he had a new car, but as a recruit he was not allowed to keep it. I had a garage that went with my quarters, so I allowed him to park it there until his recruit days were over. This team went on to be the military champs of the nation.

I was fortunate to be assigned to the unit of a Staff Sergeant named Henry Pickerell, who in my opinion was one of the best soldiers to ever serve in the Army. He was put in charge of all training of the unit. He and I teamed as color guards many times, if I wanted the best to carry the colors at the time. He was also a Virginia Country boy. We were from the same cut of cloth. More on him later.

General Pershing was ill in those days at Walter Reed Hospital, as he got worse we would rehearse his funeral often. When he passed on he was to get the best the Army could provide, and I was there to see to it. When he passed on, he lay in State at the Capitol and my men stood guard. When he was taken from the Capitol and loaded on the caisson drawn by six white horses, I was pallbearer in charge. Behind the Caisson and me came General Eisenhower, General Bradley, and four other Generals, names I can't remember now, as honorary pallbearers, but there was a picture of entire group following the caisson in the

163

Washington Paper that I have donated to the museum at Fort Myer, Virginia. As we walked across the Memorial Bridge we had a big rain shower and all got wet, but we kept going. To this day I have the white gloves I wore at that funeral.

Another interesting event that I played in was when Padereski's body was to be moved and taken back to Poland. My company Commander became ill and the Lieutenant was on leave, so I called the major in the Pentagon and informed him that we had no officer to be in charge of the Honor Guard at the grave site. He told me he would get back to me soon. Brigadier General Ferenbaugh was MDW Commander in those days and knew me from W.W.II. as he had been Assistant Commander of the 83rd Infantry Division. When the major called back he asked if there was an IKE jacket and cap belonging to the Lieutenant in his locker, I looked and stated "yes," he replied, "you're in charge, wear the Lieutenant's jacket and cap and handle the Honor Guard." I felt real good about this. When we formed at the Tomb of Padereski, General Ferenbaugh was there.

Lined up on left of casket with cabinet officers, Generals Bradley and Eisenhower and other military officers serving under General Bradley at the time. 1st Sergeant Waple top left of casket.

He wanted some information from me and called out Sergeant Waple, the Honor Guard and army band personnel cracked up. Here I was dressed as a Lieutenant which the General had approved, and yet he calls me Sergeant Waple.

During this period of time, after 1946, I had moved to better quarters, a duplex, brick up and down. During the summer of 1947-48 my wife would wheel the twins up and down the street and most people stationed at Fort Myer knew they were my offspring. As they became 4-5 years old, I would take one of the horses down to the back yard of my quarters and let them ride. The enlisted swimming pool was only about one block distance from my quarters so the twins learned to swim at an early age. I would drop them off the eight foot diving board, and they would bop back up and swim to side of pool, some people thought I was cruel.

General Eisenhower's chauffeur also moved from those inadequate quarters next door to me. He would always play with the boys as he had time.

After approximately three years as First Sergeant of the Ceremonial Detachment and experiencing many interesting moments of parading, honor guarding, and leading these units to having a reputation as being one of the best in the army of the day, I was very proud.

Before the war and during W.W.II, I either visited my Mama once or twice a week, or called her if possible. I always sent a short note or card weekly when in Europe stating that I was OK and loved her dearly. During this time at Fort Myer, after the war, I would go see her at least twice weekly. After the twins came I took them to see her every weekend. Now her baby boy had two baby boys for her to love. As soon as they could walk she bought them a pony, a shaggy looking old shetland. Mama sure loved those boys as she loved all of her grand children, but I think she liked my two more. On every visit I would take her for ice cream, she liked Breyers Vanilla the best. I would also brush her long hair that she would usually have in a bun. As she sat in her rocking chair I would stand behind her and brush. Every once in a while I would reach over her shoulder and try to fondle the mole between her breasts that all of her children had done as we nursed. She would say, "George Henry, stop that, you're a bad boy," we sure loved each other. Mama was very proud of me too. Whenever a picture of me was in the paper she would call all of the family and friends and ask if they saw her baby boy's picture in the paper. A couple of times with President Truman, once when I modeled the new uniform, at General Pershing's funeral, and once at the airport when I met the plane with an Honor Guard for the return of the bodies that had been recovered from a plane shot down in Yugoslavia.

Sometimes I would take my family up to Mama's and stay all night on Saturday. I wanted those boys to see what country living was like. One time we had put them to bed in what had been my bedroom, and soon after dark, a whippoorwill started whistling from out back in a near by tree. This scared the heck out of them, they had never heard a noise like that before. The bull frog noises from the pond also aroused their interest. I took them to the swimming hole where I had learned. It was not a nice pool like they had back at Fort Myer.

After the horses left Ft. Myer back in 1942 the riding hall was converted into a gymnasium and the Army was holding the Army boxing finals there. As I knew everyone at Ft. Myer, I arranged for a preshow of the regular matches that the twins, Grant and Gary put on an exhibition bout of three one minute rounds. This really went over big.

My sister Hazel and her hubby had a business in Washington, but lived out at Waples Mill. On the way home from work they would stop by Ft. Myer and visit. They always brought something for the boys. They bought them tricycles, red wagons, and beautiful clothing. Clark, Hazel's husband would lie on the floor and play with the twins as if they were his. I was so lucky to have a great family, and being the youngest of eight, I was also still their baby brother. I didn't do anything to disrupt these feelings either.

One day in August of 1948 I received a call from the Post Commander telling me that General Bradley, now Chief of Staff of the Army, was looking for a new chauffeur and body guard and asked if I had a man that would qualify. I've mentioned before that I had a Sergeant who was probably one of the best soldiers in the Army so I told the Colonel that I had a good man for the job. I was told to send Sergeant Pickerel down to the Pentagon the next day and report to General Bradley's office. I lost my best soldier, but for a good cause. He was promoted to M/Sergeant immediately. M/Sergeant Pickerel later married and moved into the quarters that Sergeant Dry had vacated to accompany General Eisenhower to Columbia University in New York. I had lost "Pick," as he was called as a friend, but gained him as a neighbor. He and his wife also became good baby-sitters.

After Sergeant Pickerel moved in next door his house became like a second home to the twins. "Pick" and I lived in identical houses and would display a lot of competition on who could grow the best flowers, we sure had beautiful yards. We both knew the superintendent of the Cemetery and would scrounge tulip bulbs and the like from him. We always had fresh flowers in our homes also. We would go to the dump in the cemetery and pick out all sorts of fresh flowers that had been put there from the latest funerals. Sounds horrible, but as soon as the families would leave the grave site, the flowers were dumped. They would only live a day or two, but there was always a fresh supply.

I had now been in a position of glamour for three or so years, and was very proud of this period. I had performed, in my opinion, admirably in the position. I had received lots of praise over this period, but could not help to drop a hint to my friend "Pick" that if General Bradley needed another chauffeur and bodyguard I would be available. Sure enough in a week or so he came to me and informed me that the General's Chief of Staff asked him if he knew of another person who would want the job, I jumped at the chance and was accepted. General Bradley now had two of the best men

168

in the Army on his staff.   My ceremonial and honor guard days were behind me.

Commissioning Day
12 January 1952

| **Mrs. Catherine Waple** | **2nd Lieutenant George Waple** | **General of the Army Omar N. Bradley** |

Master Sergeant George H. Waple, whose promotion was announced on January 4, 1952, received his bars from his wife and General of the Army, Omar N. Bradley, Chairman, Joint Chief of Staff.

To Lt.
with best Waple
wishes

General and Mrs. Omar Bradley

Fort Myer Virginia

WASHINGTON

29 December 1951

Dear Waple:

As you leave my office to assume your active duty commission as a 2d Lieutenant for assignment with the 5th Infantry Division, I want to express some measure of my appreciation for your fine service as my chauffeur during the past three years. It was reassuring to have in this job a fine noncommissioned officer of high ability, good moral character and good judgment. You have performed a variety of duties which extend far beyond the scope of the title of your assignment and have always been of excellent assistance to me. You have put in long hours of duty and have shown yourself discreet and trustworthy throughout your assignment.

You have been of great assistance to me and to my staff as well, and I will always be grateful for your loyalty and your outstanding performance of duty.

In your new duties as a commissioned officer I am confident that you will discharge all your assignments in the same excellent manner which has characterized your service with me.

In this new assignment and in every venture you undertake my best wishes will accompany you. I hope that you and your family will be able to be together and that you will have all the happiness and good fortune that you deserve.

Sincerely,

Omar N Bradley

M/Sgt. George H. Waple
7001st ASU
Fort Myer, Virginia

Letter from Omar N. Bradley

THE BRADLEY YEARS

On the 5th of August 1948, I reported for duty in the office of General Omar N. Bradley, Chief of Staff, United States Army. My good friend Henry Pickerel, whom I have spoke of before, briefed me on my duties so I started to work immediately. We would work on alternate days for the General and would be on stand by or on call if Mrs. Bradley needed us for shopping. Sometimes we would shop at the commissary or if she wished to go to Washington we were at her disposal. In those days I wore a blue double breasted suit with a chauffeur cap. Sometimes she would tell me to remove my cap, she never said why, but I know why, she didn't want people to think that she had a chauffeur fearing the price would go up. As much as he was a great man, Mrs. Bradley was a character. She never dressed up for shopping and wore roll down stockings that were up to her knees, sometimes falling half way down her leg. The General had a Cadilliac limo, vintage 1942, and for Mrs. Bradley we used a small Buick Sedan. For a personal car, they had a 1946 Buick. They told me that he had gotten a real break when he bought it from General Motors. It was robin egg blue and we kept it polished to a "Tee."

During the remainder of 1948 and 1949, up until the Korean War, things were generally routine. There was President Truman's Inauguration, and lots of parties in Washington. I would drive General & Mrs. Bradley to all of the parties. I remember once at the Mayflower Hotel, they came out the side door and as Mrs. Bradley got into the car I noticed that the General's Zipper was down when he walked by me as I was holding the door open, I whispered, "General," your fly is open," he got in, reached down and pulled the zipper up, and then thanked me. Mrs. Bradley said, "What are you doing Omar?"

Before the General came out Phil Harris had come out, we chauffeurs recognized him and spoke. He shot the bull with us for a few minutes.

During the summer of one of those years that I worked for General Bradley, Mrs. Bradley insisted that I take some time off and take my family to West Palm Beach where Kitty's mother and father owned a duplex. We drove to and from so we had a car to go to the beach and such, I guess the boys were three or four years old at this time.

One day I was to take him to the Laurel Race Track. Enroute we picked up Mr. Marx of the Marx Toy Company. When there was a lull in their conversation I informed them that I had a brother who was running a horse in the fifth race and that when we got to the track I would go find my brother and get the dope on his horse. This I did, and was told that the horse had a good shot at winning, was in the right spot. The horse's name was Tumble Boy and was on the tote board at 10-1. I rushed back to the box seats and told the General and Mr. Marx that my brother thought the horse would win. I left to place my bet, after the race I was happy that I had won and had given the winner to them. Upon reaching the box, excited, I said "We won." The General replied, "Yes, I bet two dollars on him." I felt like saying, "Two dollars, hell, I bet more than that." Years later, I read in the back of his book that the General had a passion for horse racing and he became a handicapper due to his mathematical talents, but rarely won. I could see why; he only bet two dollars.

Being a sport enthusiast I followed all sports as did the General. When he got in the car each morning, I had already prepped myself on the current sports events. We discussed baseball, racing, etc. He knew Ted Williams' batting average, how fast the special feature race was run, he knew it all. We discussed sports from Ft. Myer to the Pentagon. The General and I had a special feeling toward each other as I had been with a fighting Division during W.W.II, of which he knew, and of course I knew what he had done in W.W.II. I was proud to be on his staff and proud just to stand in his shadow. I think he respected me to for my W.W.II. service. As he states in his book on April 12, 1945, "spearhead units of the 83rd Infantry Division, namely my Regiment, the 331st Infantry crossed the Elbe River at Barby, heavy German pressure was present, but the 83rd Divisions bridge head held firmly and they expanded against strong opposition."

One time the General was going to the Army and Navy game with President Truman. I drove to Philadelphia with the Secret Service and met them at the station, then drove to the stadium right in and under the stands. After the game we drove them back to the train for their return to Washington. Sergeant Pickerel had taken the General and Mrs. Bradley to the station and was to meet them upon return. The two or three Secret Service men and I left Philadelphia and did not stop until we got to Washington, they drove straight thru - no stops at lights or nothing, what a trip, we probably beat the train home. The General had a small personal staff, maybe twelve or fifteen. When one of us had a birthday there would be a small party for them after hours. One time the General introduced me to Mr. A. Harriman, a Statesmen. The General knew that I was the father of twins and I had also told him that my wife's birthday and mine were on the same

175

day. Well, he got this a bit confused, he understood me to say all four were on the same date. So he was telling Mr. Harriman, you know, Sergeant Waple has twins and he and his wife's birthday are all on the same date. He told Mr. Harriman, I can understand the twins birthday on the same day and even he and his wife's being on the same day, but it must have taken a hell of a lot of planning to get them all on the same date. We could have used him during the war with that kind of planning. I never corrected the General as it made a good story. These parties soon stopped as soon as Mrs. Bradley heard the tingling of glasses and smelled the General's breath upon arriving home.

Then all hell broke loose, the Korean War. The General would receive a briefing from his staff every morning and then either Sgt. Pickerel or I would drive him to the White House for a cabinet meeting with the President. I would accompany the General with the map into the cabinet briefing room, placed the map on an easel, gave the General the pointer, and go to the back of the room. Even though I was cleared for the highest of security, sometimes, the General would ask me to step outside. But that was a great experience being present in the cabinet meeting. One time after the General's briefing, I took the map back to the car and was waiting for him, all of the sudden he came running out, and said, "Waple," "get me back to the Pentagon NOW," I was there in a few minutes, never stopped for nothing. I remember going across the Memorial Bridge at a real high speed.

Another event that has always stuck in my mind was when General Eisenhower came back to the Pentagon for a briefing on the Korean situation. After the briefing, he and General Bradley went to the White House to brief President Truman and the Cabinet, General Eisenhower being more of an advisor. The Chief of Army, The Navy, Air Force, and Marines were also present, and upon conclusion of the briefing they all walked out of the White House to my car. General Bradley invited the Chiefs to ride back to the Pentagon with him. One jumped in the front with me, General Eisenhower, and Bradley, plus one other, sat on the rear seat while the other two sat on two joining jump seats. As I drove across the 14th Street bridge I thought to myself, and a lot of time afterwards, the headlines I could have made if I had pushed the gas pedal to the floor and did a sharp right turn into the Potomac River.

During the time that General Bradley was Chief of Staff, and later as Chairman of the Joints Chiefs of Staff, I had the occasion to meet a lot of high-powered people of the day, Congressmen, Senators, and foreign dignitaries. During this time, General Bradley had started writing one of his books, and at times I would go into a small office with one of his secretaries and proofread the materiel for the book. Years afterwards when the General completed the book, I read it knowing that I had participated in it's early stages.

As time went on and the Korean War got hotter and hotter, everything was not good between General Bradley, his Chiefs, and General MacArthur. Overhearing comments and conversations I could even feel that General MacArthur was in hot water. As previously stated, in the official record, General Bradley was instrumental in General MacArthur being relieved.

After General MacArthur returned to the States there was a ceremony on the monumental grounds honoring him. As General MacArthur went down the receiving line he shook hands with all on the receiving stand, but as he approached General Bradley, General Bradley stuck his hand out, but General MacArthur ignored it, passed right by him without even a grunt. I guess he knew who was responsible for his relief even though President Truman took the blame.

General and Mrs. Bradley had one daughter, whom at the time I worked for them, had two children. One, a boy who was about the same age of my twins, when staying with his grandparents, attended kindergarten. On alternate days I would drive him there. He would ride with me up front and at times put his feet on the dash. I asked him not to do this, the next trip I had with Hank (The boy's name) I was informed by Mrs. Bradley before we took off that if Hanky boy wished to put his feet on the dash he could do so, my reply was "Yas um."

Another time Mrs. Bradley asked me to teach Hanky to swim, so we would go to the pool at about ten a.m., after several of these lessons, I took my twins with me. Hank turned me in again to his grandmother. I was told that I couldn't take my sons to the Officers Pool, all in a day's work.

On another interesting occasion I drove Mrs. Bradley and her daughter downtown Washington where they went shopping. The daughter bought a dress for a party coming up, she was tall, and in this dress she looked great. The next day after the party I returned the dress to the department store. When I told my wife Kitty this story she almost flipped. My co-worker told me that he had done this also.

Some other duties that I had beside chauffeuring was to show movies at Quarters #1 for whoever was present to watch. I had to learn to operate a 16mm projector and get the film from the library in the Pentagon. After a while of this, it was decided by someone that one of the house boys could show the movies. In those days, especially the Chief of Staff or the Chairman, were entitled to have enlisted men work at the house. There was a chief cook, an in charge noncommissioned officer, and four or five Pvts., Pfc., or Cpls. These people served meals, cleaned the house, washed clothing or whatever. They were actually maids and servants. At several of the larger cocktail or cocktail dinner parties, Sergeant Pickerel and I tended bar as some times there would be more than one bar. Once, I remember, as bartender I wore black trousers, white bow tie, and mess jacket, looked rather handsome. As the party progressed I noticed this very attractive unattached female eyeing me, soon she came to the bar and we spoke, as the conversation got more interesting she asked my name and what did I do. When I replied that I was the General's chauffeur, she split. I really got a laugh out of that, probably missed a hot date.

On those days that I did not work for the General, I had to stand by, as I said before, for Mrs. Bradley. Sometimes when we would go out in the mornings, and if we came home by midday, and she was going to remain home for the rest of the day, I would be free to be with my family. However, sometimes Mrs. Bradley would not make up her mind as to her intention until maybe 1 or 2 p.m. then call and say she wanted to go shopping or was going to stay home. Once in awhile, no call at all and we wasted a day sitting around the house. Of course, I did have the twins to play with.

As time passed by Mrs. Bradley and I didn't see eye to eye more and more. She favored Sergeant Pickerel, she called him "Picky." It was always "Picky" this and "Picky" that. One time he was stopped by the MP's for speeding on the Fort. The MP's Lieutenant was called, as Sergeant Pickerel told the MP who had stopped him who he was and who he worked for, the Lieutenant came and told Sergeant Pickerel that he didn't care who he was or who he worked for. Well, when "Picky" got to Quarters #1 and informed

Mrs. Bradley of this, all hell broke loose. I am not sure to this day if that Lieutenant has returned from the North Pole.

Before the Korean War came along General Bradley would take Wednesday afternoon off and play golf. He was an avid golfer. I would take him home about noon, and drop him at the front steps of Quarters #1. I would then pull the official car to the rear of the house, go inside get the keys to his private car and his golf clubs. By the time I returned back to the front steps he was out and ready to roll. He could really change his clothing quick. Very rarely would I drive him to the golf club, he felt it was an unofficial trip. I remember once the General was invited to Augusta for golf and vacation. Sergeant Pickerel and I drove his private car from Ft. Myer to Augusta, stopping enroute at his old home place near Hurt, Virginia. His Mama and Papa were living on an old peanut farm. The house was similar to the one that I was raised in, very primitive. When we arrived at Augusta, we met the General at the local airport as he was flown down in a C-47. The General took the car and we flew back to Washington in the C-47 after the General's vacation he drove back to Fort Myer.

As time went on and my relationship with Mrs. Bradley got worse, General Bradley told me that either he or I had to go. He said, "I can't go because I am in charge of the entire military forces, but I'll tell you what I going to do, I'll promote you to 2nd Lieutenant and send you on your way."

He promoted me in his office on January 12, 1952, gave me a great commendation and personal letter. I even got a sweet note from Mrs. Bradley with my first set of Lieutenant bars. I always had mixed feelings about this, but I guess it was for the best. "Picky" stayed until General Bradley retired. Then he went from one C/S to the next, staying at Ft. Myer for about 25 more years. He retired as an E-8 and stayed on in Washington DC working for the Government. He did good, married a nice lady from South Carolina and is now living in a beautiful home in Dillon, South Carolina.

Even though rank has its privileges, many officers took great pride in introducing themselves with their rank preceding their name. I had lived with this policy all my service years; however, there was one man who really impressed me once or twice, and once in particular. I was chauffeuring Five Star General Omar N. Bradley back to the Pentagon and as we got to the Memorial Bridge circle there were several cars that seemed lost. The General stated, "Waple, pull up beside that car," with this he put his window down and stated, "I am Omar Bradley, can I help you?" Usually the folks in the car were very surprised to see the General, in fact, so surprised that they could not answer. He took great pride in doing this. I was proud to be a part of it.

7TH ENGINEER COMBAT BATTALION
(LEADERS' COURSE)
5TH INFANTRY DIVISION
INDIANTOWN GAP MILITARY RESERVATION, PA.

20 December 1952

SUBJECT: Letter of Appreciation

TO: 1st Lt George H Waple, 0963868

1. I wish to express my appreciation for your excellent performance of duty during your assignment to Leaders' Course. I particularly wish to cite the manner in which you have performed the duties of Tactical Officer and later as Chief of the Military Training Section. Your high sense of duty, supervisory ability and energetic and enthusiastic attitude has done much to bring credit on the Fifth Infantry Division Leaders' Course.

2. Needless to say it is with regret that our relationship is severed. If at any future time our paths should cross, I would very definitely desire your service in my command.

3. I wish to add my well wishes for continued success and good fortune in your future assignments.

RICHARD L COHEN
Major Infantry
Commanding

This officer is one of the most outstanding 2d Lieutenants I have ever known. His performance of duty is superior. He possesses initiative drive, willingness to work and a spirit of getting the job done quickly, quietly and efficiently. Little or no supervision is needed when he is assigned a job. His bearing and soldierly qualities are outstanding. He is the type of junior officer the Army is looking for. Military life is his life. His loyalty to the organization is of the highest. I would fight to get him as a unit commander under me.

I greatly desire to retain this officer under me if he is promoted. He is not pending courts-martial.

2d Lt Active Reserve from date of appointment, 21 Oct 48 to day preceding call to EAD, 10 Jan 52 (Regular Army, Enlisted Man).

TYPED NAME, GRADE, AND ORGANIZATION OF RECOMMENDING OFFICER | SIGNATURE OF RECOMMENDING OFFICER
RICHARD L COHEN, Major
7th Engineer Combat Battalion

182

COMMISSION

Now a 2nd Lieutenant

On January 12, 1952, upon receiving my commission, I was now a second Lieutenant. I didn't even know how to spell Lieutenant on the 11th of January, now I was one. I took some leave as I had to pack my household affects and move Kitty and the twins back to her home in New Jersey. We stored the furniture. I reported to Fort Benning, Georgia, after my leave for the basic Infantry course. After being a First Sergeant during W.W.II, and the soldiering at Fort Myer, post W.W.II., this course was a snap. I finished in the top ten percent of the class. This course lasted three months. After graduation I stopped by the Pentagon and visited with the General, Colonel Mathews and other members of his staff. Mama was still living at this time at Waples Mill so naturally I visited her and I got a big hug and kiss. A few years ago I was her freckled-face baby, and now I was a Lieutenant in the U.S. Army. After a few days upon returning to New Jersey, and visiting with my wife and twins who were living with my mother-in-law, I had to report to the 5th Infantry Division located at Indiatown Gap, Pennsylvania, a few miles north of Harrisburg. The 5th Infantry Division was now a training unit preparing soldiers for combat in Korea.

I was assigned to one of the thirteen battalions. Training was for thirteen weeks at each battalion so there was a graduation each week, and a new training battalion beginning each week. The Commanding General, Major General George Barth, had a policy that each second Lieutenant take a week course in leadership at a special formed leadership battalion just for this purpose. This battalion also trained out selected enlisted men in leadership for purpose of becoming non-commissioned officers. As previously stated, I was in now my fourteenth year of soldiering so there wasn't really much the course could teach me. I finished number one among my peers and was retained at this unit and placed on the faculty as Chief of the Military training section. A Major Richard Cohen wrote of me as being the most outstanding Lieutenant that he had ever known, he further stated that my performance was superior. I was promoted to First Lieutenant. Soon after that I formed a silent drill platoon that performed at special parades and ceremonies. The platoon went through a series of moves without command, I called it a silent drill. I got a real nice commendation from Lieutenant General Carter, Corps Commander of the area.

As stated, there were thirteen Battalions in training at all times. In a Battalion, there were one thousand men. General Barth liked to see men parade to music. The division band had only thirty-seven men so could best split into two bands and play at two different locations. The General did not particularly like the dress of the musicians and came up with the idea that in addition to the bandleader and a Warrant Officer, there should be someone to shape these bands men up. He had his G-1 call the leadership Battalion Commander, Major Cohen, and requested that he furnish the General with a Lieutenant who could straighten the group of musicians out. I was selected, and reported to the General's Aide, who escorted me in to meet General Barth. Upon reporting he asked "Where have you been, and what have you done?" I can see that you are not a child. Well, when I finished telling him my history, he stated, "You're the man I want." He told me what he desired in addition to getting hair cuts and shoes polished for band members. He also wanted to form a Drum and Bugle Corp. The band size could not be enlarged because of Army regulations, but the forming of a Drum and Bugle Corps could have no restriction as it would not be on paper.

Platoon at Indiantown, PA for the General 1952, Second Lieutenant Waple Commanding.

Upon reporting to the band barracks I received a cool reception. The Band Master and Sergeant in charge were happy as they were. I used diplomacy, tact, and a friendly approach. I told them I was not there to harass them but to help. I convinced them how much better they would feel if they looked better. All went well, I attended band practice and got to know all of the musicians. There was one

Sergeant First Class, Sergeant Harrison, a drummer, who impressed me the most. I told the Band Master that I would use this Sergeant as my man in helping to form this Drum and Bugle Corp. As each new group of men reported for recruit training, about one thousand were greeting in one of the large theaters. After everyone finished their orientation speech I got up and told them who I was and what was happening in my area. I asked if there was anyone who could play a "C" note on any instrument to report to a certain place at a certain time. Of the thousand men, I got about one hundred who wanted to join my Drum and Bugle Corp. or the band. Of this one hundred, I would pick approximately ten men who could actually play some instrument.

I did this every week, soon we had twenty, thirty or so men who would report at 3pm every day to the band rehearsal hall. I went to Chicago and bought bugles, then to Philadelphia to buy taberts that hung down from the bugle with the 5th Division Insignia in the middle of it. Sergeant Harrison was selected to organize the groups and did a fantastic job. It wasn't very long before we were playing big time music throughout the Division. With the regular band and bugle corps band split we could have music in four areas at one time. General Barth was as thrilled as was I. In addition to running the band I was his personal aide. I would report to him every morning at about 9 am, and we would ride throughout the division area, it was big. Soldiers in all phases of training were all over marching, manual of arms, rifles range, and I felt good being with the General through all of this. At times when we would walk by a drilling company armed with the M-1 rifle, I would notice that the fifth man in the 3rd squad of the first platoon had his rifle tilted a little. I would bring this to the attention of the General, he then would walk over to the company

Commander and tell him what I had just relayed. I would see that the company Commander was confused, as well as impressed, with the General's knowledge of close order drill. I was an expert on close order drill, manual of arms, guns, formations, and parade procedures. Remember, I had helped write the manual after the war back at Ft. Myer, Virginia when 1st. Sergeant of the ceremonial detachment. I really made points with the General.

I did this until the spring of 1953, at which time I received orders for Korea. When I received orders for Korea, the band held a big farewell party for me with the General being there. I was presented another commendation for a job well done.

I got housing at Indiantown Gap in the spring of 1952, I moved my wife and twins to that area. I found a three-room apartment in an old farmhouse nearby, we had two bedrooms and a kitchen. It was in the country and nice, the twins loved it as it had lots of space and an old barn to play in. The twins started to school in the fall and took the bus that came by the gate of the farm. Kitty had them dressed beautifully as they would leave. Being identical, we dressed them alike. One day the teacher got provoked at one of them and stood him in the corner. Upon completion of his punishment, the teachers said, "now Grant, let this be a lesson to you, his reply was, "Me not Grant, me Gary" The teacher told us this story and felt very embarrassed about it.

I had to take them out of school when I received orders for Korea and move them back to New Jersey. Upon entering them in school in Farmingdale, it was disclosed that they had not learned too much in Pennsylvania and had to repeat the grade.

I had to leave them again, I bought them new bikes before I left, took them for an airplane ride out over the ocean, and made an agreement with Connie Russel, owner of an ice cream store in Farmingdale, that if they ever came in and looked like they wanted a cone to give it to them. If I did not return so be it, and if I did I would pay up. On my return a year or so later I went to Connie and asked how much I owed him, his answer was, "George" you don't owe me a nickel," I was happy to be part of such an agreement.

Time came, and I was taken to the airport in New York by Kitty and her brother Paul. It was a late flight so I had said good-bye to the boys as I tucked them in. It was a sad evening.

I arrived in Seattle, Washington and reported to Ft. Lewis replacement depot. I received whatever processing required and got on a US naval ship, the Marine Lynx, for Japan. The last evening in Seattle I got robbed and had to wire my wife for money until I got paid again. Played poker going to Japan and won a few dollars. I didn't land in Sasabo, Japan broke. I arrived at the replacement depot bedded down with others. We received additional training in use of firearms and were briefed on the Korean situation daily. I remained at Sasabo, Japan for a week or so and upon reading the bulletin board one day I saw my name instructing me to get eady to roll at 6 a. m the next day. I also had been assigned to the 7th Infantry Division, and at this time, was in the thick of battle with the Koreans and Chinese.

Upon reading this notice, I called a cab and went to the dock where one could buy a bottle. I purchased a fifth of VO and was driven to a hotel on a mountaintop. I selected a companion, had a few drinks and dinner. I then was given a nice massage and bath with instructions to have me a cab ready at 6 a.m. the next morning. If I was going to be killed soon I wanted to be clean.

Being the ranking officer that was going to the 7th Division I had a roster of a few more Lieutenants and about fifty enlisted men. We got on a small boat and landed in Puson, Korea.

Author tying a scarf for Marilyn Monroe, Korea 1954

KOREA

Battalion Adjutant

George with children of orphanage

General Taylor, General Bryan, General McGarr and LT. Waple

190

Lt. Waple, USO Lady and General Mcgarr

Designated escort for
Marilyn Monroe "USO" tour

1st Sgt. Lynch and LT. Waple

191

KOREA

Upon landing in Puson we boarded a train. There were replacements for other Army Division's plus the Marines. As we rode North in the dark, I could see what I knew was artillery fire flashes. The train stopped some time later, and an announcement was made for all men going to a certain Division to get off here, on we would go. Soon the artillery flashes got closer. The train would stop and the announcements continued. This went on until we passed the artillery flashes and only my group only was left. Soon the train stopped and I was told to unload. When I got off, I noticed that there were no more tracks, and a large smoke stack with a Cavalry insignia painted on it. I loaded my men onto trucks and we drove off into the dark. My safe days back in the Pentagon kept running through my mind. What have I done, why couldn't I have kissed Mrs. Bradley's butt more often. Oh well, someone had to be there and this old country boy was it. I was proud to be a part of it even though I did check my neck for my dog tags.

We drove for a time and the truck stopped. I was told to take my men and follow the Sergeant. All of the officers, six or eight of us, were told to bed down in that tent. At day break we were told that breakfast was being served. I recognized a few other officers that had left Fort Lewis with me, they had been there for a few days. Between meals we loafed, played horseshoes, or read. One by one the other officers in the tent were summoned to pack up, we shook hands and they left. In a few days I was the only one left. Man, I thought to myself, maybe they have lost my records and have forgotten me. No such luck, in a day or two more I was called by a Lieutenant from Division. He introduced himself and away we went. I was assigned the 31st Infantry, it was strange; I had been with the 331st. Infantry during W.W.II. As we arrived at the right Command Post I was taken to the S-1, a captain, strangely enough, he too had been on the boat over from Ft. Lewis. As we greeted each other he had my records in front of him. I was being assigned to the 3rd Battalion, but before I left the Regimental Commander wanted to see me. I was shown to his office and introduced. His name was Colonel Doleman, a good looking West Point officer, class of '33. I noticed his ring and told him that I had served with a classmate of his while working for General Bradley. I wanted to make as many points as possible. He noted from my records of my past, with this he stated that I was to report to the 3rd Battalion Commander, a Lieutenant Colonel Merrill. Upon doing so, luck was still with me as I had known Colonel Merrill back at Ft. Myer, Virginia when we both were Master Sergeants. He had been riffed back to M/Sergeant from a Capt. after W.W.II, but had stayed in the reserves. He had been promoted to Major in the reserves and when called back on active duty he became a Lieutenant Colonel. His greeting was cordial, and informed me that I would be assigned to "L" Company as its present Company Commander was being rotated. I was taken on a tour of the Battalion front the next day, shown the trenches, barbed wire, dug in tanks, mortar position, the enemy lines, and a desolate area of real-estate between the front lines, wasn't a very attractive place. As my luck was still with me, the next day, Lieutenant Colonel Merrill called me to his Command Post. He knew I had been a First Sergeant and knew administrative work. He told me that I outranked all of the platoon leaders of "L" Company, but could not give me the Company because one of the platoon leaders, who had fought well,

193

deserved the company. I couldn't have agreed more. He further stated that his Battalion Adjutant was ready to rotate and that he was going to give me his job. Well, I didn't show too much emotion, but I could have really kissed his butt for making this decision. I was ready to be the best Adjutant in the whole U.S. Army. It was a great experience, however, being in the Battalion Command Post at night and hearing by radio that all hell was breaking loose, the front calling for artillery fire and motor barrages, a real chill ran down my spine when I heard they are in the trenches with us, not a very pleasant report.

A few months later the truce was signed and we pulled back. The 31st set up tents at Camp Casey. The line companies would rotate every week back up front in the trenches, but there was no fighting. We just watched each other over this vast empty acreage. Many of the officers and men who had served their time were being rotated, actually faster than replacements arrived. The officer strength was to a point when only one or two officers were left per company. When the regiment pulled back to Camp Casey and we got settled in our tents, I had a tent put up for the officers club and built a bar out of scrap lumber. As the officers rotation became more rapid, I found myself all alone in the officers tent. I had a cot with double mattress, mosquito net, a home made chair, homey like. I also had a piano like wire strung around my corner tied to several tin cans. Sometimes we would have visitors during the night looking for anything they could steal. I kept my 45 pistol under my pillow just in case the cans rattled. There were paths in the near by brush that our guests would use during their travel at night.

On one summer day, 1953, our Division Commander was being replaced by a Major General from the prison of war command. Upon arrival, there was a requirement for someone to become his aide-de camp. Notice went out through the Division units that if there was any Lieutenant who wanted to apply could report to the Division headquarters on a certain date. When my friend, who had come over from the States with me and was the Regimental Adjutant, called me and asked if I knew of anyone that could report, I asked who was the General, his reply was Major General Lionel McGarr. Lady luck was still with me. I told the adjutant I would apply for the job as I had known General McGarr when he was a Colonel at Ft. Myer back in '45-'46. He had been a Regimental Commander in the 3rd Infantry Division in Italy, during W.W.II, and after the war he was being held over at Ft. Myer waiting for the next war college class to start.

My Company Commander at the Ceremonial Detachment, a Capt. Ross Calvert, had served under Colonel McGarr in the 3rd Infantry during W.W.II and when the Colonel was at Ft. Myer doing very little, he would come to my company and visit with Capt. Calvert. I would serve them coffee and sometimes arrange for filet steak and eggs. This went on for quite a while and I got to know the Colonel pretty good, he too could see that I was a veteran of W.W.II and ran a good show.

When I reported to the 7th Infantry Division G-1, there were about twelve or fifteen other Lieutenants there. A few wanted no part of being an aide so they were dismissed. The rest of us, about ten as I recall, reported to the General's hut. Upon arriving, the present aide lined us up in alphabetical order so I was last in line as it had been all my life. When the men went into see the General they would be in his office anywhere from three to five minutes, next, and so on down the line. Finally me, I walked in looking my best, clicked my heels and saluted. I reported, "First Sergeant George Waple reporting sir," in my best command voice. This took him by complete surprise and it took him a minute or two to recognize me. It had been seven years since we had seen each other. The General jumped out of his chair shook my hand warmly and said, "What in the hell are you doing here?" With this, he pushed his buzzer to summons his present aide. When the aide came through the door, the General said "I got my man," I want you to meet an old friend, George Waple." I got the job, another lucky day for George Henry. When I reported back to the battalion and informed the new battalion Commander who had just replaced Colonel Merrill, he was provoked. I packed and said good-bye Major, see ya around.

Here I was, a high school drop out, an old Lieutenant of 33 years of age, the aide to the Commanding General of the 7th Infantry Division. Another proud day for me, but yet, it wasn't too far out of place as I had at one time, not many years ago, been on General Bradley's staff, and at the 5th Infantry Division, General Barth's assistant. So I think I can handle this job, but the best part was the living conditions, I was uptown again. Headquarters of the 7th Infantry Division was at Camp Casey. The previous General had had his engineers build a stone building that was used for a mess hall and lounge. At one end of the lounge was a beautiful fireplace, and on one side wall was a bar. The dining room was about 30 x 60 feet with one long table. In normal attendance there would be from twelve to fifteen people that were on the General's staff. After I got settled in it was not long before I was running the show. The Mess Sergeant would coordinate the menu with me deciding what we would eat, and how it would be served. The Mess Sergeant had his cooks and six or eight mess boys.

To fill up the table, but mostly to get the General to know the leader's of the Division, I would invite four or five guests for each dinner meal. These guests would come from the regiments, artillery or other support units. We would have cocktails before dinner in the lounge by the fireplace. We had a group of Red Cross girls attached to the Division so I would include several of them each evening just to add a touch. Also, when we had USO troops traveling by I would invite them to dinner. There were Slappsie Maxie Rosenbloom, The Ink Spots, The Wings Over Jordan Group, Roscoe Ates, and others. Sometimes these groups would have a few very attractive ladies present.

It would be quite an evening, 20-30 people present at times. I also obtained the birth dates of all of the staff, and on their birthdays there would be a cake or when one of the staff was going home we would have a going away cake in his honor, any excuse to have a party. Captain George Patton, the son of General Patton, was attached to the 7th Division with his recon group. The General had a party and a cake when he left the 7th to rotate back to the states. I have several pictures of Capt. Patton cutting the cake.

Most of the General's staff were West Pointers and at first I had a tough time breaking the ice with them. I remember one time after I first became the General's Aide, his C/S, Colonel Bastion, Class '33, gave me some advice on what he expected of me. After all, who was I, with no formal education being in a job like this. I just dazzled them all with foot work, and really the only man I had to keep happy was the General, and I did in my opinion, do just that. I believe the General thought so too. There wasn't a thing that he wanted that he didn't get. When he said pass the ice cream after dinner, I was the first one to laugh as we had no ice cream. It wasn't long after when we did have ice cream. I went to the Quarter Master and requested that they come up with a solution on making ice cream, hell, it was not long before we had peanut flavor, good too. A policy I set forth was that some members of the General's staff would offer the blessing at every evening meal. I assigned this duty out each day prior to taking out seats.

One reason I believe General McGarr chose me to be his aide is that he had seen the job that I had done back at Fort Myer, and from the report his friend, Captain Calvert, had given him of the job I had done as First Sergent, and what an outstanding soldier I was. I had served with many outstanding soldiers, in war and peace, and in my book I was one of the best. Book learning or no book learning I always tried to instill in every soldier that he should believe that he was the best soldier in the US Army.

The General liked an old fashion bourbon before dinner, in fact, two most of the time, but I soon learned that two was his limit and I would cut him off. This became a favorite joke of his, he would say after two, well ladies and gentlemen, we may as well eat as my aide won't allow me to have another drink, again all would laugh. The General was a good man, West Point Class '28, gone through the army schools, led a Battalion, and later led a Regiment into battle with the 3rd Infantry Division. At beginning of W.W.II, he fought in Italy under General Mark Clarke who approved of his style, as I was told later by General Clarke when he was visiting Leavenworth. Among his other medals he had a chest full of Purple Hearts, he had attended the War College after the war, after his Fort Myer days.

Every day he would go on an inspection tour somewhere throughout the Division, but most of the time it was at the DMZ. I would coordinate with the G-3 and select a place for him to go. If he could fly in via helicopter he would. I would arrange for the chopper to pick him up at headquarters as we had a landing pad nearby. I would take off by jeep and meet his chopper at a pad near where the unit was that he was going to inspect, we would jeep in or sometimes the pad was close enough that the General would walk, he loved to walk and walk fast. One time we were met at the bottom of a big hill, and the Regimental Commander and Battalion Commander were there. After reporting, the General would say, "lead the way." About half way up the trail, the General and I passed the Battalion Commander, when we got to the top and the Battalion Commander caught up, he was relieved of his assignment. I felt sorry for the poor soul, a Major who had just came over from the States, was out of shape and didn't last long. When the General inspected the position's riflemen, machine gun position, and mortor positions he would ask questions and make comments, I had learned "pig" short hand and took notes.

On return to our headquarters, I would dictate my notes to a clerk who would type them. The General would read my comments, make whatever changes he wished, and then passed them onto the Chief of Staff for publication to the Regimental Commander.

It was a chore keeping up and taking notes, and being in a position to hear the General's comments. We had a few Hispanics in those days and most of the time when the General asked what his mission was, the reply would be, no speeky English. As the General was fluent in Spanish, he would repeat his question in Spanish, even then, some could not understand pure Castillion Spanish. Not only had the General been raised in Yuma, Arizona, near the Mexican Border, he had majored in Spanish in school. Needless to say, the poor Spanish soldier and his squad or platoon leaders had to correct this problem soon, it may not be too serious that the soldier couldn't speak English, but he must know his field of fire and mission. There was another problem that the

General soon straightened out, the term "Bug Out," it had to be abolished from the front line troops. There would be no "bugging out" term used in the 7th Infantry Division.

The 7th Division was deployed in the right center section of the DMZ. General McGarr and I walked the entire front, he had the experience in battle and was tough. Everyone must know their job, if not, they would not be around long. To shore up the trenches and bunkers on the DMZ helicopter would hitch onto 10x10 timber and fly them to the top and almost place them on exact spot they were needed, this was some task. I guess some of those timbers are still there.

Can't forget the Korean people and especially the kids, when they would have to defecate they would just go into a rice paddy or field and go. I have several cute pictures of kids doing this. Speaking of kids, Christmas of 1953, I had asked my wife back in Farmingdale, New Jersey to send boxes of anything, food, clothing, toys etc. to me. I have a photo of about 25 or 30 boxes I received and presented to the pastor of a Methodist Church and the kids, my wife got everyone in that town to send me something.

After the hostilities, the 83rd Infantry Division moved back to an area called Camp Casey. I became connected to a children's home and more or less adopted about a dozen of them. I had my wife send clothing from Farmingdale, New Jersey for the girls at Christmas of 1953. We had a great time sorting clothing for each girl. I was a good Santa Claus and made all the young ladies happy. It was another gratifying moment of my life.

In addition to being a hell of a soldier, leader and Commanding General of the 7th Infantry Division, General McGarr was also a camera buff. Everywhere we went and everything we did was photographed, I must have taken thousands of pictures. He wanted pictures of terrain, churches, Budda temples, whatever, and if he could be present he would be in the photo. One picture that he wanted in particular was the Port of Inchon. This was the area that no one thought General McArthur could succeed in pulling off a landing there. Our troops pulled it off with great success because as General McArthur preached, the element of surprise would be in his favor.

One time General McGarr was invited for dinner by a lady who was the President of Ywa Womans College in Seoul. I took a quart of IW Harper for beverage and as we ate, dog, seaweed, and kimchea, I would immediately take a sip of IW Harper. We sat on the floor and were accompanied by the Lady President and four of her prettiest young ladies, nice evening.

During the fall of 1953, and up until the General and I left Korea, there were many USO and VIP visitors. Sloppsie, Maxie, Rosenbloom had a great troop, two young ladies especially, both from Utah and about 6 feet tall, they were gorgeous. I have a photo of these ladies standing beside Lieutenant Colonel Wright our G1 with his arms around their waist and grinning like a mule eating briars. At dinner, I always sat at least one beauty by the General. We had a policy that all of these visitors would become honorary members of the 7th Division. The General would pin the Seventh Division hour glass on each of them with my assistance, it wasn't all work. Another VIP was Cardinal Spellman, his group arrived on a very cold day and he wasn't dressed appropriately. I was wearing a parka with hood when we met him at the helicopter pad. Upon seeing that he was going to be cold, I removed my parka and helped him put it on. I never got my parka back and a few years later when visiting him in New York with General McGarr, I mentioned the parka incident to his Holiness. He said that he remembered and that he still had it, and was going to keep it too.

We had dignitaries from Congress, the Pentagon and foreign countries, I have pictures of most of the VIP and USO troops. There were singers, dancers, and comedians, but the most important USO troop was Marilyn Monroe. She was accompanied by Mrs. O'Doul, wife of Lefty O'Doul, the baseball pitcher and a friend of Joe Dimaggio. I arranged their living quarters to be near the General's mess. There was a stove, two cots, and several chairs. I met her at the chopper pad and escorted Marilyn Monroe and Mrs. O'Doul to their hut.

When we got inside I briefed them on our plans, and that I would be back to escort them to dinner. In her group was a Department of the Army USO representative whom I coordinated everything with, and then there were other tag alongers. When we arrived inside her quarters, Marilyn Monroe sat on the cot and asked me if I would remove her army issue combat boots, the ones with the buckle, naturally I said yes. When I got them off she asked if I would pull her GI trousers off, at this moment I felt my blood pressure rise. As I removed her trousers I discovered that she had on long johns, this is as far as I went.

I had invited, with the General's approval, certain people who might enjoy Miss Monroe's company. We had a full house and a lot of photos were taken, but the main photo was a picture just of her, autographed to me, George Henry. It was stolen from my home years later. I have one of her talking to Joe Dimaggio on the phone. He was in Tokyo at the time and I got through to the Army at Seoul, Korea and over to Tokyo where he was staying. I have a photo of me holding the Army field telephone with Mrs. O'Doul looking on. There was a great party, every one had a nice evening.

We had a big cake with all of the trimmings. The DA USO representative that was accompanying Miss Monroe, sitting to my left at dinner, was a real jerk.

He criticized the fun we were having and wrote a horrible story about our party that did not clear 8th Army Headquarters. The Chief of Staff to General Taylor, 8th Army Commander, was a classmate of General McGarrs', and upon seeing this release called General McGarr really excited and asked what in the hell happened at Marilyn Monroe's party? Nothing happened, we were just having a party. This DA USO rep was relieved from his duties upon returning to the States, but there was a Corporal from the Army Times who wrote of this party and other events that happened throughout Miss Monroe's tour. He wrote a news release years later saying that he was sorry that he did not come to the aide of the DA USO individual who wrote the story of which was mostly a publicity stunt made in poor taste. The article appeared in a California publication and I refute any and everything he wrote pertaining to the 7th Division. No one got drunk or patted Miss Monroe on the butt.

For Miss Monroe's visit I had two Army issue wool shirts made up with Division patches, insignia, and other Division momentous, I had one for Miss Monroe and one for Mrs. O'Doul. The General presented them the shirts and I helped the ladies put them on, lots of photos were taken again. I then tied a blue Infantry scarf around their necks. Marilyn stated we were beautiful and she was having a ball.

The next day I took Marilyn Monroe on a jeep tour of the Division area allowing all the soldiers to see her. She waved kisses and shook hands with many of them. More photos were taken, she was beautiful. That night there was a show, and I went to her hut in a sedan we had borrowed. She and Mrs. O'Doul got in the back seat and I sat in the front.

As I looked at Marilyn Monroe from the front she was sitting on the edge of the seat as the dress was very tight. She was wearing a black sequin dress, and was stunning as well as gorgeous. I am not sure if there was anything else other than the dress. With this dress her breasts looked beautifully full.

That press release not only told of our party, but about every other place Marilyn Monroe went. He stated that some Generals were patting Marilyn Monroe on the butt, etc. I know for a fact that my General did not, I was there, and in complete charge. Marilyn left a day or two later, but I have beautiful memories of our relationship even though it was short lived. As I write this I have the photo of Marilyn Monroe and I standing in front of a fireplace. I was a happy camper.

It so happened that the shirt Marilyn received was brought home and given to Joe DiMaggio's son. Evidently he didn't care too much for it as the shirt was still hanging in Joe DiMaggio's first wife's closet upon her death. The first Mrs. DiMaggio had remarried to a man who is the brother of a lady who now has the shirt. I'll bet Joe, Jr. wishes that he had it now as it has to be worth a lot of money. This lady has a hobby of collecting mementos of Marilyn Monroe and really has more pictures of her trip to Korea than I do. In fact, she traced me from my photo and called me several years ago asking if I was Lieutenant Waple, General McGarr's Aide.

I will go on record at this time, regardless what anyone ever says about the Marilyn Monroe's party, it was just a fun party and no one ever patted Marilyn Monroe on the butt, or ever got out of line.

In May 1954, General McGarr departed Korea for Japan and a new assignment. As Commanding General, US Army Carribbean, he asked me to accompany him. We were homeward bound.

Captain Patton cutting his farewell cake on his departure from the 7th Division, Korea

Lt. Waple
Korea, 1953

Lt. Waple getting a hair cut
Korea, 1953

Aide de Camp
Army Caribbean Command (1954-1956)

| 1st Lt. | Mr. & Mrs. | BG & Mrs. | 1st Lt. |
| George Waple | McGarr | Laidlaw | McDaniel |

1954
(below, left to right): President Royas, Pinella Columbia; MG L.C.
McGarr, USA Charge Deaffairs, 1st Lt. G. Waple

Lt. Waple
Korea, 1953

Lt. Waple
Korea, 1953

"Riding with the Gauchos"
Mauricio Verdier Ranch
Mato Grosso, Brazil

Lt. Santos Republic of Cuba, 1955

MG L.C. & 1st Lt. G. Waple greeting the Ecuadorian Ambassador to the Canal Zone and the Minister of Defense

CANAL ZONE

After leaving Korea, I accompanied the General to Japan staying in Tokyo for a few days, then flew to Travis AF Base, California. I got General McGarr on another plane to join his wife and family then went to the operations officer and scrounged a flight on a military aircraft to Washington as a courier. It was a bucket seat on a C-54 I believe, not comfortable, but cheap. From Washington I took a train to New Jersey after visiting my Mama for a few days.

General McGarr's next tour of duty carried him to the Canal Zone, Panama, as Commanding General U.S. Army Caribbean. He asked me to join him and I gladly responded, affirmative.

Arrangements were that we would meet at Ft. Hamilton, New York with our families for the voyage. I made all arrangements and was in New York when he and his family arrived. We boarded the ship with our first stop being San Juan, Puerto Rico. As that commander was a Brigadier General, and fell under the jurisdiction of General McGarr's new assignment, we received great VIP treatment. We were shown all around the island and given a party.

We arrived at our destination after going through the Canal to the Pacific side and were met by the Commanding General, General Whitlock, and some of his staff and aides. General Whitlock's Aide de camp's wife corralled my wife and twins as I had to remain with my boss. When arriving at Ft. Amador, General McGarr was given a Honor Guard with his general staff to be and dignitaries from thereabouts. A cocktail party followed with General Whitlock, his aide, a Capt. Little, General and Mrs. McGarr, my wife and me.

After the party we were escorted to our billets that were set up for immediate housekeeping, food, wine and beer in the refrigerator. My quarters were on the second floor of a four unit complex over looking the bay on the Pacific side of the Canal Zone, it was beautiful, especially on a full moon night the moon rays shining on the water reflecting up through the palm trees. This country boy was in high cotton again.

There was a transfer of Command and General McGarr took over. There were many briefings and greetings. The General's office, as well as mine, was on the second floor with a porch over looking part of the golf course and parade field, it was very nice.

The General's secretary was a carry over, an older gal, but fun to work with. She knew the ropes, protocol, and who to watch out for. Once I made a statement to her that I'd lay her 8 to 5 that a certain thing would happen, her response was, "That's an odd hour." As General McGarr got adjusted he called on the Commander in Chief Carribean Command, Lieutenant General Harrison. His headquarters were at Quarry Heights with most of his staff under a mountain top, not really a mountain, a big hill with a tunnel which was built for safety during the war. General Harrisson was a fine officer and gentlemen, very religious too. I met Vice President Nixon at a party held at his home located on this big hill.

All of the Ambassadors located in Panama called on General McGarr soon after his arrival to present their credentials. The General had to call on the President of Panama to present his credentials. This country boy was still on a roll. The General and I had to have white dress uniforms tailored, a blouse with white trousers, and a white mess jacket for formal wear. Wasn't too long ago that I

212

didn't know what a white mess jacket was, now I am wearing one.

The US Army had a military mission in every country in Latin America, except Argentina.

A mission was comprised of from one officer and a couple of enlisted men, to several officers and maybe ten enlisted men. Their mission was to educate the local government on Army procedures. At that time many of the Latin Countries were very primitive. General McGarr would visit these countries to pay respects and to inspect our people stationed there. He would take a staff plus a doctor on all trips. I had the job of coordinating these jaunts with a Colonel who had the title of Mission Chief on the General's staff. For local trips in Central America we might visit two or three countries on a trip. Usually we were housed in a hotel, but sometimes with the local country mission chief, The U.S. Ambassador to that particular country, or sometimes as the guest of the President of the Country we were visiting. For trips to Chile, Paraguay, and Brazil, we would be gone for a week and had a converted B-17 to fly in. For local trips we used a C-47. In those days we had to carry oxygen, and if we flew over 10,000 feet would have to use an oxygen mask. For instance, the airport in LaPaz, Bolivia was itself at 10,000 feet. LaPaz, the Capitol of Bolivia, was almost two thirds down the mountain, so once there breathing was OK.

One time we went from LaPaz to Cochabambaha as the mission to that country was split. The airport runway there was gravel and upon landing the B17 sounded as if it was going to fall apart. Another time the pilot got off course and we flew up the wrong valley. Upon recognizing this, he had to fly against one side of the mountain and bank the plane very steeply, the plane was almost in a stall and was vibrating like crazy, but we made it. When leaving this airport, the pilot had to pull up fast as there were mountains in front, in doing so the tail wheel dropped down hitting the gravel and blew the small tail section tire. We were heading for Peru and tried to fly over the Andes, with this altitude we had to use our oxygen mask. We ran into a storm and tried to go around it, no dice, and had to return to Cochabambaha. On landing with the tail tire flat, I thought the entire tail section of the plane was going to break loose. All went well however, we stayed overnight, got the tire replaced, and the next day flew on to Lima, Peru.

Lima was nice even in those days. The General, his wife, and I stayed at the U.S. Ambassador's home while the staff went to a hotel.

I remember that after I got General and Mrs. McGarr in the living quarters, there was a short time for rest before the evening party. I was shown to my room by a servant, and as I laid on the bed I saw a sash cord by the head board, I thought, what's this. So I pulled, the next thing I knew there was a knock on my door, I said, "Come in," it was a servant, he said, "You rang, sir." I was astonished, but didn't want to sound too country so I ordered a beer, this country boy was uptown again. While in Peru we were taken on a trip to the Inca Ruins, it was some sight. I still have a leg bone I picked up just laying there on the ground.

Uraquay was also a bit primitive as was Paraguay and Ecuador. When we went to Brazil we circled the monument of "The Christ of the Andes." The Rio beach looked beautiful from the sky and even more when I was on the sand. The beautiful ladies were ever present. From Rio we went to San Palo taking a few days vacation to visit a large cattle ranch owned by a Brazilian who had married a lady from the US.

The ranch was located in Central Brazil, a place called Motto Grosso, and was huge. Our host had a large home with guest houses on each side. I lived in one of the guest houses with the air crews. There were thousands heads of cattle and in one photo I am with ten gouchos (cowboys) mounted. Being an old Cavalryman I could sit a horse. I was dressed as one of the gouchos in their custom cowboy uniforms, looking just like one of them. I rode with them one day for awhile. The ranch had an out post every mile or so to monitor the cattle, it was a sight to behold.

Another time our host took us on a boat ride down a river that ran through his property, as we drifted along alligators would slide off the banks into the water and/or they did so I would shoot at it with a high powered rifle provided by our host. At the time I thought it was a great sport, but now that I think about the shooting, I find that it was cruel. I would not do it today. I have another photo of our host where we were both dressed in a goucho uniform and boots, great photo.

Another time we landed in Trinidad, the plane was met by a donkey and cart to secure our baggage, that was cool. That evening at a formal dinner we were entertained by a steel drum band, they were different and also very good.

I cherish the photos I have of these trips through Latin America. I have one where I was meeting the President of Ecuador, the President of Paraguay, Costa Rico, and Nicaragua. If we didn't meet the Presidents, we would meet their representative either from their cabinet or the top ranking military Generals. The President of Nicaragua's son had graduated from West Point, I believe Class of 1946, and was now Chief of Staff of their Army. We had with us on my General's staff a Major who was a classmate of this young man. I have one photo of me as I was taking a picture of the Presidents palace in Lima, Peru where we were entertained. Columbia really put on a great show honoring General McGarr, I was happy to be a part of it. In addition to visiting Venezuela, General McGarr was sent there by the State Department and DA to negotiate an arms deal with their Government, we were there for a week or so. In addition to work, I had an enjoyable time.

When I was not traveling with the General, I would in addition to my regular chores try to spend sometime with my twin boys. They were in the Boy Scouts at Ft. Amador and met once a week. Each week the troop would be inspected by an Army Officer for appearances, posture, and speech. I taught them good, either Gary or Grant would win every week. My wife had them neat as a pin and I taught the military stuff, such as the salute, and how to stand and a talk if asked a question. I was very proud of them. They remained in the scouts whenever they could. At Ft. Leavenworth one progressed to Star and the other to Life, then we moved on. I have a picture of them at Ft. Amador, and my eyes tear when I look through the albums.

Fort Amador, which is on the Pacific side of the Canal, is right on the water. There was a "Q" boat that was available to the General which normally was used by the enlisted men to justify its existence, but at any time the General wanted to use it, it was available. One time I reserved it for the weekend and took friends and wives fishing. There was a Captain and crew including a cook and mates. If someone caught a fish it would be taken off the hook by one of the ships mates. Upon arrival back to the shore, the fish would be wrapped for each family to take their share.

The General wasn't an avid fisherman, so if a VIP or an Ambassador wished to go fishing over the weekend I was designated to be the host. It was a tough life, but someone had to do it. To make any trip official all I had to do was invite a foreign dignitary and then I could write it off as an official trip, shady, but that's the way it was done in those days. On one trip as everyone was resting bottom side, I was sitting in the big chair at the back of the boat. The Captain yelled, "Sail up" and about that time he struck the middle pole. As I was already in the chair one of the mates strapped me in. Twenty three minutes later I landed a 156 lb. sail fish, the largest one caught in 1955 in that area. We donated it to the children's home. I have a picture of that catch, by looking at the photo, I see that I had taken some of the General's family out that weekend and to justify the trip the Ambassador from Peru was along.

About two hundred yards from the Army HQ was the Navy HQ. An Admiral Miles, (two Star) was General McGarr's counterpart, Navy wise. He and his wife were great. The admiral had an aide of about 6'1", dashing and handsome, his name was Jack Galanor, as I recalled, and was from Hollywood.

After his tour of duty in the Navy he retired to California and the movies, his movie name was John Gavin and later in years he became Ambassador to Mexico. He spoke fluent Spanish was a bachelor and had some great parties at his quarters at the Navy housing area. He had his own house, not a BOQ, always had several beautiful Panamanian ladies around. He is probably still living in California as he was younger than I. After he departed, the admiral and his wife had to visit Brazil. As he didn't have a replacement aide, my boss loaned me out to the Navy, it was a nice trip. Admiral Miles and his wife were sweet people. The Navy wasn't as demanding as the Army.

As I look through my album I see one picture of my wife and I in the most formal attire. The photo is annotated that we were going to a party at the El Panama Hotel and hosted by the President of Panama, this Country boy was still up town.

The President of Guatemala was invited to visit the U.S. by President Eisenhower and the State Department had selected General McGarr to accompany the President to the States. I had to go to keep everything in order. By this time General McGarr had become very dependent on me. We took a plane from Panama and flew up to Guatemala, picked up the President, and flew to Miami, Florida. We were met there and flown to Washington in President Eisenhower's plane. The President of Guatemala and General McGarr were quartered at the Blair House. As I wasn't on the list of VIP's no consideration was given me to stay anywhere, but in General McGarr's suite, there was plenty of room so I made out OK.

After getting the President and General settled in and coordinating everything with the secret service, I called my older sister Hazel whom I adored. When she answered the phone and I announced myself, she said, "George Henry, where are you?" I proudly said, "Down on 16th St. in the Blair House," of course she was thrilled and excited. What are you doing there? I then told her the entire story. That evening there was a State dinner being given by General Eisenhower in honor of the President of Guatemala. General McGarr was his interpreter and companion and was at his side at all times. That evening as I recall, it was a black tie event, I assisted my boss in getting dressed and down to the President's suite where we met the secret service who would drive the President and General to the State dinner. I tagged along and ate in the kitchen, but found it an interesting evening. The next day we went to New York City and lodged at the Waldorf Astoria Hotel. I found a room with the secret service. The first evening after I saw the General to bed, I went down to the night club. Upon entering the door I was confronted by the head waiter. I was dressed in pinks and greens and looked sharp. I told him who I was and what I was doing there, with this he said follow me and I did to a seat in the front row center. I enjoyed the show and felt this country boy is still strutting.

Sailfish caught by me 1955 Canal Zone off Q56 Army Boat. Pictured with captain of boat.

The next day the President and his entourage called on Cardinal Spellman. When I went through the receiving line, introduced myself and reminded him that he took my parka back in Korea, he laughed and told me that he remembered and that he still had it, that was fun. The President visited many sights of New York, including The Empire State Building. As we were on one of the high levels of the Empire State Building, I was taking pictures for my boss. I had two of his cameras strapped around my neck. To take one picture I had to take the strap from around my neck and when I finished this particular photo, still thinking the strap was around my neck, I released the camera. It fell down to the next tier smashing the telephoto lens. This didn't set too good with my boss so the next day I took the camera to the Army photo lab in Brooklyn to have the lenses repaired and camera checked. The bent lens housing was all that was damaged, thank God. I don't recall how long we were in the States, but we did return to Latin America namely Ft. Amador without further incident.

It was sometime during the year 1955 that I got a call from Rufus, my brother, that Mama had had a stroke. I flew home, but later I assessed this trip home as a mistake, as when I reached home I found my loving Mama the sweet beautiful lady looking so pitiful, a sight that I have never forgotten. When I had last seen her prior to shipping out for Panama during the summer of 1954 she had looked like the Mama that had given birth to me, nursed and coddled me all of my life. I guess I reacted properly about going home and General McGarr insisted that I do so. I hitched a flight out at the Air Force field in the Canal Zone to Florida and took a commercial flight from Miami to Washington. The following year I got another call from the same brother telling me Mama had passed on and was joining papa in heaven. I had just completed coordinating a long trip throughout South America and had the complete itinerary planned, including who the General would meet and every minute detail. As we were to leave the next morning I told no one of my brother's call, not even my wife. As I look back I still feel that I made the correct decision, what could I do, Mama was dead, I didn't want to see her twisted face that had been so beautiful again.

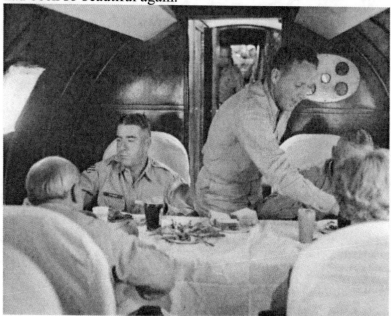

Serving lunch to General McGarr and staff on B-17, enroute to South America 1955

I think we were in Chile when I told General and Mrs. McGarr of her death. At first he scolded me for not telling him, and I am sure if I had, he would again insisted that I go home, but later when I explained my excuse, he acted as if to understand.

It was on this trip that Mrs. McGarr had a birthday and while in Santiago, Chile, I called ahead to our next stop, a place where the U.S. Army Mission to Chile was located and arranged with the Mission Chief to have flowers at our arrival for Mrs. McGarr and at the dinner party that night to have the band play Happy Birthday as we all sang. Mrs. McGarr never forgot that birthday, we often talked about it later.

The General attended a missile school in El Paso, Texas during the summer of 1955. He and I, along with two pilots, flew up to Ft. Bliss, Texas in a C-47. After being out of the States for sometime now I craved some cantaloupe with vanilla ice cream in the center of it.

The pilots and I visited Juarez Mexico several times when I was free. The General had a good friend stationed at Ft. Bliss, so had dinner with them several evenings, those evenings I was free. In one nightclub in Juarez where we went there was loads of ladies, as we sat there having a beer I found myself entranced by this one female who had the largest bosoms I had ever seen. When she noticed me gauging, she said, "The way you are looking you probably would like to see them all." She then lifted them right out of her dress and laid them on the table, what a sight, we finished our beer and left.

Several days after our arrival I called the nurse's quarters of a U.S. Army General Hospital nearby. A maid answered the phone and I told her who I was and what I was doing there. With this she told me to call back around 4 p.m. and ask for Capt. what's her name, I called and got this lovely voice on the phone. I told her who I was, what I was doing at Ft. Bliss and that I had two handsome pilots with me. Her answer was, "two friends," I will pick you up at the Ft. Bliss Officers Club at seven p.m." Sure enough as we sat on the porch of the club up pulls this new beautiful yellow Ford Victoria Convertible with three females, we knew these ladies had to be our dates. Well, I can tell you now, why they

222

were free, they were the ugliest women I had ever seen before in my life, not young chickens either. They were so ugly they would stop you in your tracks, in fact, they would have stopped Big Ben. After introductions we had them in the club for a drink, I am glad no one knew me. We then took a pleasant ride through El Paso, and surrounding areas, stopped for a snack, returned to the Fort then thanked them for a nice evening and said good night. I was surprised to see them the next evening as we had indicated that we were low on funds the night before, but low and behold the next evening the pilots and I were having supper at the club, and who walks in, but these same gals. We greeted them cordially and bought them a drink. After this, another ride in that beautiful car, top down and me driving. These ladies were as proud as peacocks it appeared, they had corralled three handsome dudes. Before we left Ft. Bliss for the Canal Zone, I believe we saw most of Western Texas and parts of New Mexico, they sure filled in the down time with tender loving care.

The General was also called to Washington for an Army Commander's conference. I was delighted as I was going home for a short visit.

The boss would be tied up all day and at lunch times, so I had time to visit my sister, brothers, and friends. We were billeted at Ft. Myer, my old home base of many years. It was wonderful, the place where I had joined the Army and had served after W.W.II. It was also the place where I had met General McGarr when he was a Colonel, we talked of those days. Once when walking down a corridor in the Pentagon with the General, we met an old friend, Major General George Barth, remember, I had worked for him at Indiantown Gap, Pennsylvania, the place where I put together a drum and bugle corps. General Barth was so surprised to see me, and when I introduced General McGarr to General Barth, General Barth said, "You know McGarr, you have one of the best officers that I ever commanded working for you." General McGarr replied, "I know it," and I am going to keep him too." It was another time when this country boy felt ten feet tall.

Our trips to Cuba were nice, that was before Castro. There was one nightclub in Havana that was outstanding. They had a great show and our seats were right up front. These show girls were the most beautiful I had ever seen, having not been to Vegas yet. The Cuban Army assigned an aide to my boss to assist me in all of the events. He was a dumpy little guy but nice, spoke fluent English and really showed me the sights after I tucked the General and his wife in.

In the meantime, my family was having a ball too. The twins met many kids their age and played till dark every day. They went to school in the Canal Zone at a US Government facility. Kitty being a nurse got a part time job at the Canal Zone Hospital. That and our social life kept her busy. The boys also like to fish off the causeway.

My routine was walk to the office, about two blocks, sort the correspondence, mail or whatever, and be ready for the General when he was chauffeured to work by a great young man, M/Sergeant Pheiffer. He was a jewel, always on time, knew the ropes, and was a great deal of help to me. On the General's arriving out front he entered the building and went up the stairway to his beautiful office. I would meet, greet, and brief him on the days activities. If there was no official luncheon he would go home and rest, as at times the heat was unbearable, returning to his office about two p.m. There would be official cocktail or dinner parties, three or four times a week. Changing uniforms, trying to stay dry and neat was a problem as hardly any place had air conditioning. At home one would have to remove the sheets from the bed and place them in a closet with a heating element to keep them dry.

Sons, Grant and Gary, ready for Cub Scout meeting. Panama, 1955

In formal dress, attending party at Panama hotel.

I played golf whenever I could, but it got so that my group would deny me the pleasure as most every round the General would send a house boy to find me with instructions to go to the office and get a paper that the General was working on. This was a real chore. You see, the golf course at Ft. Amador was all around his house, and I was never more than a minute or two away. I guess that went with all of the charm of the job. I was left handed when lefties were looked upon as out of place. In fact, I bought a beautiful set of Pro Line clubs, bag, and cart from a Lieutenant who also was lefty, but was sold on being a righty. I got everything for $100.00 and kept them for years, teething on them becoming as low as an eight handicapper years later at Ft. Monmouth, New Jersey. My first handicap when established was 18, from the fact I believe was that I was a good hitter in baseball.

As our tour of duty was coming to a close and the General had his new assignment announced, which was to be the Command and General College, Ft. Leavenworth, Kansas, he asked me if I want to accompany him, but I declined. I was getting a little fed up with this type of duty never knowing when there would be free time. I asked to remain at Ft. Amador for another year and be assigned to Headquarters Company, a housekeeping unit at Amador. This was arranged for me by the General with stipulation that if all didn't go my way I would be sent to Ft. Benning, Georgia for the Infantry Advanced Class.

After several weeks, before the General's departure, there were many farewell parties, military and civilian, throughout the Canal Zone and Panama. Finally the day came, I had him all packed and the furniture had been shipped to Leavenworth. It was really a hectic month doing this chore the way the General wanted it done.

The afternoon of November 30, General McGarr accompanied by Mr. William Barber, American Charge d'Affaires, paid a courtesy call on Columbian President, General Rojas Pinlla. (L to R: Waple, McGarr, and Barber).

I received good support from all agencies concerned, but over the past two years of doing my job, the way it should be done and done to satisfy my boss, I had stepped on a few toes of officers who worked for the General. After getting the General and his family on the ship, as they were sailing back to the States, I went home, took my shoes off, and had a drink.

Lt. Waple being decorated by Major General Lionel C. McGarr at headquarters, Canal Zone, 1955.

Within a week after the General left, there were rumors that I was being transferred to the Infantry stationed nearby for a jungle duty. I immediately went to the G-1 of personnel and requested the Infantry school assignment. Being a good man, he kept his promise to the General, and cut orders for me to report to Ft. Benning for the fall class starting in September. It also coincided with the public school dates. So I packed my family and sailed home landing in New York City and met by my wife's brother when the ship docked.

**General McGarr, with Waple (right) Farewell speech
Canal Zone.**

USA AGAIN

The furniture was shipped to Fort Benning, Georgia After some leave visiting our relatives in New Jersey and Virginia we drove on to Georgia. Upon arriving, we immediately started seeking adequate housing and found an apartment near the main gate of Fort Benning. The apartment was very satisfactory, in addition, many of my classmates were living there. The twins were enrolled in a near-by elementary school that they could walk to and from.

The Advanced Infantry School was much tougher than I expected, I really had to study. Most of my classmates were professional career soldiers of the regular Army. I was back in the real Army again. I became good friends with several other Captains who lived in my complex that were regular Army, they were my salvation. In addition to hanging out with them, we studied together. They also accepted me like a brother and respected me, I believe because of my W.W.II and Korea experience. We would swap homes for study periods each evening as all of us had children. During these study periods we would use the entire dining room with our books, maps etc. One of these gentlemen, whose name was Middlestadt, was brilliant, in fact, he finished number one in the class at graduation. He was my special tutor.

On arriving at Fort Benning, I soon discovered that Colonel York, my W.W.II. Regimental Commander, was Director of Instruction at the Infantry School. As soon as I could, I paid him a visit proudly wearing my new Captain bars and combat Infantry badges with star. When I arrived at his office I checked in with the secretary and asked her to announce me as his First Sergeant from W.W.II. As I walked in, he was pleasantly shocked to see me, not a First Sergeant, but a Captain. We had a long chat, fought the war over, and had a couple of good laughs. It so happened that he was having a cocktail party the next evening and invited me and my wife. He took me around and introduced me to every single person at that party. We talked about our mutual friend, Fred Barnes, and many others. It was an outstanding evening for me seeing him again, I also bragged about his performance during the war. I had heard from Barnes that after I left Germany to come home that he became friends with the beautiful blonde Hungarian lady that I mentioned previously. He asked me to come by this office Monday morning and instructed me to report to him each Friday afternoon and brief him on the weeks presentations of his instructors or anything else I cared to comment on, I was honored to do so.

With all of my military experience I had, not had any real formal education, my study habits suffered and my high school drop out days came back to haunt me. My father once told me, when in doubt, use common sense. With this advice and Capt. Middlestadt, I would make it.

Because of the class room work, there was little time for golf as I had to keep my nose in the books.

After my many years of service and the great officers that I had served with over the years, led me to have friends in high places. So prior to graduation I had contacted an old friend stationed at the Pentagon and got assigned to the Military District of Washington, located near the Washington National Airport. When I arrived with my family back in Fairfax, Virginia, I stayed with Sister Lucy who had bought the old home place at Waples Mill until we found a house. My brother Raymond knew of a split-level new home in the city of Fairfax that was reasonable, and that he would help me buy. I had some collateral and he signed a note for me so I could buy. The price of this three-bedroom split level had a living room, kitchen, dinette, and den was only $21,000. Today the same house would sell for two hundred thousand. We moved in and I started to drive to and from work, but soon found a car pool. I had been assigned to the G-4 section of this headquarters as a maintenance officer. I had a civilian co-worker who showed and taught me the ropes.

My office formed inspection teams and inspected all units that fell under the jurisdiction of this headquarters. Some of the units were as far away as Fort Churchill, Canada, on the Hudson Bay. I had several interesting trips there, one or two in the summer, and at least one in the winter. It was cold, in fact, in the winter time one could not stay out of doors for any length of time. During the summer it got up to about thirty degrees, so it was bearable. I took a helicopter ride over the bay to watch polar bears and the lakes to see thousands of geese. All of the garbage from the Fort was dumped at the edge of the bay so the bears had a feast. Couldn't do that today, I don't believe.

The duty I was performing kept me busy, but was not too interesting. I worked for a West Point Colonel who wasn't the sharpest Colonel. There was also a lot of repetition in the job. We would inspect, write a report, and brief the unit that had been inspected, pointing out good and bad points.

My twins were not in little league at Fort Benning so on arrival at Fairfax, I checked on the league and got them signed up with a team in last place. They didn't get to play too often as the manager of the team had two sons on the team who couldn't play very good. I became a coach and tried to get my boys into the game, which wasn't too often. Therefore, I started to point out to the manager that the best players were not getting to play, namely my boys. I had

232

played baseball and knew the game so I began to tak
this really provoked the manager so we had words. He f...ally

conceded and stated, "If you're so good, you manage the
team." Well the season was almost over and this team
finished in last place. There also wasn't one kid who had a
complete uniform. The next spring, 1957, I was named
manager and got a couple of 1st draft picks. I really worked
my team hard practicing plays, hitting, fielding, and all
aspects of the game. I would have my wife meet me at the
practice field after work with the kids and a change of
clothing. The other parents brought their boys also. I had a
rule to all parents that if I was going to teach baseball, one
parent must be present at all games, this was my policy. I
had brothers on the team who had not hardly played at all last
year, but there was a rule that each boy must play so many
innings, that was good. These two boys were the sons of a
distinguished attorney in Fairfax, John Rust. His Granddad

had been in the State Senate, also a lawyer and they were wealthy. The Rust boys became a project for me. I asked their father for assistance as there was no money for uniforms. He responded, took my list of what we needed and went to Washington and bought it all. On opening day there was a ceremony at the best field near the American Legion. The teams walked onto the field in order that they had finished the previous year so my team was last. I had two assistants, a Navy Commander and a Colonel in the Army, but I was the boss. My team didn't straggle onto the field, we marched on with bright new uniforms, boy did they look good. Not another team had a complete dressed group as mine, we had rehearsed and were in step. I brought them to a halt and right face, parade rest, everyone in the stands applauded. We had a good season, finished in first place with one twin at first, the other in the outfield. The boys of the previous manager were transferred to another team. Not only did we finish in first place, I received an award as manager of the year. In 1996 I visited Fairfax, one of the Rust boys is running for the State Senate, the other a prominent lawyer, and their Dad retired.

I almost lost one twin, Gary, when he began to choke one Sunday morning when we were at church. I rushed him to the Army Hospital at Ft. Belvoir, and being that it was a Sunday there was only a skeleton crew on duty, no one could find a doctor. I asked, where is the surgeon in charge, and was told that he was on the golf course. With this I picked up a phone and called Mrs. Eisenhower at the White House and reminded her who I was and my problem. It was only a few minutes later the doctor was there and operated on Gary. He had a tracheotomy and would have died soon as he was already blue. Another time it was good to know people in high places.

During this assignment I played very little golf because of the expense, I had the equipment, but green fees were too high.

During the period that I lived at Fairfax, I had time to share with the twins who were now eleven and twelve. I showed them the old swimming hole, the tree that we had a rope in, and then took them hunting several times where I had hunted as a boy. I explained about the mill, the dams, and the mill race. I showed them my great grandfather's original home that he bought in 1861, where their ancestors were buried, and the two room school house where I learned to color. I also told them about the out house and fox hunts. They were now old enough to understand and seemed interested enough to ask questions. They are now fifty-nine years of age and remember those early years in Fairfax.

During this assignment my wife Kitty, a nurse, took a job at Fort Belvoir, Virginia. It was about a twenty-mile ride and she worked the eleven to seven shift. She got home just in time to see the boys off to school, and I would get them up for cereal before I left for work. This left them alone for about an hour.

Naturally, this was another new school for the twins, they were now eleven years of age and been to five different schools. This had not worked in their favor and they were having a hard time in reading. We sent them to a remedial tutor that helped some, but I think they had a dislexia problem, they never learned to read really well.

It was during this assignment that I received orders to attend an atomic explosion in the Nevada Desert. I was flown to Las Vegas on a commercial flight, and upon arriving was loaded on a Government bus and driven to a camp in the desert. The blast was scheduled for the following early morning hours, but as that time approached we were notified that the wind was not favorable and the blast would be postponed until the wind changed. The group was notified that a bus was scheduled for the city of Las Vegas later on that morning and that we should check the bulletin board at the bus station for further instruction. I had taken a sport shirt and trousers just for such an occasion, so grabbing my toothbrush and razor, off I went to see the sights. I first located a cheap room near the bus station for three dollars per night, left my toilet articles and headed for the Golden Nugget. I was amazed at the action and food. Walking around observing the slots, games, and food, especially the prices of the food, I decided to have a shrimp lunch. I ate a ton of them only for a few dollars. I only had twenty-five or so dollars on me so had to watch my expenses, but finally decided to test my luck at a two dollar crap table. In an hour or so I was shocked that I could have won about one hundred dollars. I quit and took stock of the situation - here I was in Vegas, the wind blowing in the wrong direction, hell, I may be several days. I had a cheap room and downtown in those days breakfast was eighty-nine cents. After strolling around for a while I came upon a low limit poker game, a seat was open so I joined in. Food and drink was on the house, as were the interesting stories spoken by my fellow competition. I sat in this game for about twenty-four hours only to get up for toilet visits. Playing "close to my vest" I held my own but then decided as long as I was in Vegas I may as well see the rest of the town.

I headed up the strip gawking at the casinos - picking out one, I strolled into one, found a seat at the bar just like city folk. Nearby was another chap in the same boat as I - here for the shoot. After some conversation we noticed two beautiful ladies across the bar - told the bartender that we would like to buy them a drink, they accepted and it was not long before we were seated near them.

As it was mealtime we asked the ladies if they would like to join us for dinner. They accepted as we soon found out they were in the same boat as us, new in town.

After dinner at a cheapie joint downtown, we caught a cab and headed back up the strip. I had twenty or so silver dollars in my hand and was flipping them back and forth from one hand to the other. The gal seated close to me asked if she could try my action. I gave her the silver dollars and after a few tries she decided to put them in her purse. I said, "Hold on here gal." Give me my money back. With this she said that she would like to keep them. I agreed with the stipulation that we go to her place. With this proposition she denied my request. I asked the cabby to stop - demanded my silver dollars and asked her to get out along with her friend. We drove off leaving them somewhere on the strip.

Checking back at the bus station, we found out that the blast was on for the next day. We caught the bus, got to bed for a short while. About four a.m. we were up, on the bus headed for the desert. Into a slit trench, told to stay down, and close to the front wall, "Boom," a beautiful sight as one could witness. Back to camp and airport and Washington DC. All in a week's work.

The really one good thing of this assignment was that I was home among my sisters and brothers. I used to visit them all on a regular basis as I was their baby brother. My brother Raymond and I would have breakfast every Sunday morning with our sister Hazel. Boy, could she cook, I never forgot those pancakes, bacon, sausage, biscuits, jam, and honey. Hazel was a real doll. I hunted and fished with her hubby, Clark, several times during this stint.

One day during the summer of 1958 my secretary, yes, this country boy had a secretary, answered the phone and said, "Captain Waple, it's for you." When I answered the phone a voice said on the other end, "George, do you want to go back to work for me," it was General McGarr. The job I had as I stated before was not the greatest so with out hesitation, I said, "Yes sir." He informed me not to mention this call to anyone, that I would receive word from the Pentagon. I was thrilled, called my wife and told her. In about an hour my boss, the Colonel, called me on the intercom, "Waple, get in here." I walked down the hall and went in, he said, "What in the hell have you done," I have instructions to release you immediately, I saluted and stated, "Good-bye Colonel."

There was one nice period, probably took a week or so where I was assigned to sit on a general court martial at Fort McNair in Washington. It so happened that my boss, Colonel Glatterer, was also to sit, in fact, he was the ranking member of the jury, I being the junior member. A Master Sergeant was being court marshaled for misconduct while stationed with the U.S. Embassy in Moscow. The Colonel and I didn't agree on what sentence should be rendered as the Sergeant was found guilty, so I got into some trouble over this as he tried to pull rank with me over this important decision. It was good that I was leaving. His prejudiced feelings reflected in my efficiency report that he had to make on me upon my departure.

George's Birthday

Happy 40th Birthday, George!

MG LC McGarr presents golf trophy (Division "C" won with a 97) to new golfer Captain George Waple.

Grant and Gary Waple get personal touch from "JOLTIN JOE"

240

Lt. Sloan, assistant aide to Waple and General visiting from Canada.

Captain Waple introducing V.I.P. to General McGarr

Medal Board

FORT LEAVENWORTH, KANSAS

In August of 1958 when I received orders for Fort Leavenworth I had to sell the home that I had purchased two years ago. Because of the haste involved, I sold it for the complete pay off price, about the same as I had paid for it.

We drove to Kansas in a 1956 Mercury that I had bought in Panama very cheap, arriving there on a very hot August day.

General McGarr's present aide set my family and me up in temporary quarters, in fact, in the old type style barracks that had been converted into living quarters. There was no air conditioning so sleeping was unbearable. We lived here about a week or so when permanent quarters became available. These quarters were on Meade Ave. on the bank of the muddy Missouri River, a real beautiful spot and about two blocks from the office.

General McGarr was now the Commandant of the Command and General College, a place where every officer had to go if he ever wanted to get any place in the Army. The student body in those days, as I recall, was about three hundred and was divided into sections of about fifty each. Most students were regular Army with great potential, beautiful wives too. A couple of days after we were there the General had us at his home for a nice dinner. He introduced me to his enlisted staff with whom I would be working with.

As the senior aide I had all kinds of assistance. The General's secretary, Miss Smith, had been in the office of the commandant for years. She knew the ropes and was a sweet nice Catholic lady, thirty-six years of age and had never been married. M/Sergeant Pheiffer who was also in the Canal

Zone was the General's chauffeur, Lieutenant Sloan who had the distinction of being the goat of his class at West Point, and four or five enlisted men at the General's quarters. One of these men who was off duty was photographed while washing the General's daughter's car. Who ever took the picture had to be a "Whistle Blower" as the picture appeared in a magazine. The General got a call from the Pentagon and I had to swear by endorsement that this soldier was off duty and in passing picked up a towel to wipe the car off that Mary Louise was washing.

Mary Louise was the older of the General's two daughters. She had met a young man in college that she was to marry soon. I had the task of setting up this entire wedding to be held at the chapel with the reception to follow at the Officer's Club. With the assistance of the club officer we really put on a show, complete with band, flowers, food, seating, the whole ball of wax. This young man may have been a college graduate, but he had the common sense of a jackass. I had to lead him around by the hand. I even had to take him to the drug store for the necessities required for a newlywed, plus giving instructions.

My twins were now twelve, but still in Little League. I immediately signed them up so that they could finish the year out. They were assigned to a team again in last place. I told the coach of their talents so in their first game Gary was placed in center field. Back at Fairfax he had not made on error all year, but now as the first fly ball was hit to him, he misjudged it for an error, I felt terrible. I also signed them up for the Boy Scouts and rifle team. There was a very nice indoor twenty two-caliber range where they became good marksman gaining the highest competitive goals.

The boys started to school at the junior high located on the base. I settled into my job, which was more hectic than any had been before. I attended classes daily with the General as he inspected the instruction. He was interested that these future Generals were getting the best. I would coordinate with the director of instruction daily to work out his schedule for the next day. It was good for me as I was receiving top of the line information on tactics and other Army procedures.

The social life was good, especially during the holidays. All of the students could bring their families and lived in Government quarters. There would be section parties and the General was invited to every one of them. Some nights we would attend a cocktail party with one section and dinner with another. I had to keep a schedule of every party so that no section was overlooked. There would be a receiving line at these parties so that every officer and his wife got to meet General and Mrs. McGarr. When the General would have a party at home for someone of importance from Washington, we would invite the local mayors of the surrounding communities. Departments of the Army of the representatives would visit the college and give talks to the classes. Two of the most interesting ones were Strom Thurman and the German Scientist Werner Von Braun.

I began to get some golf in and this is where I became proficient in the game. There was a group of about twenty that would play every Saturday and Sunday, if I was free, I would be there. We played with handicaps so every one had a chance. One particular Saturday and Sunday I shot a seventy-four and seventy-five, I won a few dollars that weekend. Another time, a Lieutenant General from Fort McPherson, Georgia was coming to give a talk to the class. His aide called and told me to set up a competitive game for the General and to have a bottle of good bourbon around. I got two of our top golfers from the faculty and myself, I was to be the General's partner. When we got to the seventeenth hole the match was all tied, and I had a side hill twenty foot putt for the win. The General looked at me and said, "Boy you had better make that putt." I was nervous as hell, but canned the putt. We tied the eighteenth and won the match. He told my boss, General McGarr, about our game over dinner that night.

Duty was good there and I was happy. Kitty and the twins were happy as they too were doing their thing.

During the winter, in addition to the scouts and rifle range, there was a community center with a pool, pool tables, and ping pong. The boys met a bunch of good boys and girls there. One boy, Peter Shoomaker, followed his father's foot steps and became a General. He now has four stars and is chief of staff of the U.S. Army.

I took care of the General, as he liked. I also had an assistant, the West Point Lieutenant, who handled the household chores. He took care of Mrs. McGarr's wishes, as did my wife at times.

There were many off-post parties that I accompanied the General and Mrs. McGarr to. I met many great looking ladies with a couple being real beauties that I admired a bunch.

One cold snowy day the General was having a party in honor of someone. It so happened that Joe DiMaggio, who had retired from baseball, was now a representative for Delmonte Food Products who sold to Army commissaries. On one particular day, while visiting Fort Leavenworth, we had been at the commissary and met Mr. DiMaggio who was accompanied by a Quarter Master General from Fort Lee, Virginia. Later on that day the snow became deep closing the roads to Kansas City where Joe and his party were to catch a plane. When I realized this, I asked the General if I could invite DiMaggio's group to the party as there would be some absentees anyway due to the snow. He said great, it will add some flavor to the party.

During the party I asked Mr. DiMaggio if he would sign a couple of balls for my sons. He said sure, with this I called home and told Grant and Gary to bring a couple of baseballs to the General's house. This they did and we all went into the kitchen with Joe sitting at the table, the twins behind Joe with him signing the balls. The picture I received was a four by five, but I had it blown up to an eight by ten later.

Thirty-five years later I decided to ask Joe, now in long retirement, to autograph this picture and he refused. I pursued this just to see if I could in any way get him to sign the photo. I called his agent in Florida and was told that Mr. DiMaggio does not sign anything without pay. I have a friend of a friend of Mr. DiMaggio who said he could get the picture autographed, he too failed. In 1995 I took a grandson to the old-timers game in Yankee Stadium. After the game I went to the exit where Joe was leaving from. I confronted him about our past acquaintance of him signing the ball and how we had scotch on the rocks at the General's party back in Fort Leavenworth, the whole ball of wax. Even reminded him of how I had gotten him on the phone to his former wife Marilyn Monroe back in Korea. His response was, "I've heard and seen enough of that photo, don't bother me," and drove off. He may have a great reputation, but in my book he was not a very nice person. I just had to get the above story told, so now back to my other task.

One of the General's daughters, RoseAnn, was attending college in Ohio. Graduation was near and General would naturally attend. Prior to his departure, one of the houseboys had been promised by General McGarr that he would be

247

transferred to Europe. General McGarr called Washington and arranged with the G1, an old class mate from the point of

<u>Captain Waple's E/R - 13 February 1959</u>

A well-built, erect, military appearing and acting young officer. During his twenty years of service, he served under such officers as Generals Patton, Collier and Bradley in the noncommissioned officer grades. Being quick to pick up their good points and being highly motivated to the service, he has continually improved himself over the entire period of his service. He is definitely "old army." This officer did an outstanding combat job in Korea, as well as an outstanding job as my Aide. He went with me to the Caribbean Command where he was invaluable in my many social duties and travels throughout Latin America on missions of inspection. He adapts himself well under varying conditions, is forceful though tactful and works with minimum supervision. He employs outstanding initiative and possesses the facility of isolating the crux of a problem and taking action which brings results. He is hard working, conscientious, and continually strives to improve himself and do a better job. After field duty, I again requested him as my Aide-de-Camp here because he has the capacity of acting as an executive officer. His handling of arrangements for the heavy social schedule, as well as official visitors schedule here, has been of the same high caliber as his previous duties of this nature in Latin America. He is possessed of a fine personality, meets people well, is well liked and respected by all with whom he works, is physically capable of performing in wartime the duties of his grade and branch and has high moral standards. His family is a definite asset to the Post life, being active socially and in Red Cross Volunteer work. Because of this young officer's great potential value to the service, I recommend that he be assigned as a student to the United States Army Command and General Staff College as soon as practicable, and that he be considered for promotion ahead of his contemporaries.

transfer. This was a personal favor for the young soldier from the General, as he loved to do such favors for any soldier. While General and Mrs. McGarr were at Lake Erie College orders came from Washington transferring the young man. My junior aide, who handled most household affairs, received the orders and without telling me, rushed to the house telling the young soldier that his request had been approved. The next day on the General's return to Leavenworth the first thing he learned was about the orders from the houseboy. Needless to say, the General was provoked, as he had wished to inform the man himself.

Well, the next morning as I greeted the General when he entered his office, he flew into me about the soldier hearing of his transfer approval. I was stunned and denied that I was aware of Lt. Sloan's actions. The General still provoked gave me hell, I was the senior aide and responsible for Lt. Sloan's conduct. A big mistake, but I held my ground to we argued with me leaving his office and going home. In a few minutes the Chief of Staff was at my door telling me I must return to the office and apologize to the General for walking out. Another mistake, but I said hell no. I did not know that Sloan had received the orders and gone to the house to tell the houseboy. I too was provoked. This went on for an hour or so with the Chief of Staff going back and forth between the General and me. The day closed and I did not sleep too good that night as I figured that I would be relieved the next day. As morning came, I went to the office as usual. When the General arrived I entered his office as usual, saluting with a "Good morning, sir." His first comment was, as General Robert E. Lee told Jeb Stuart at Gettysburg for not showing up for a few days, "Waple you are a good man," I admire your courage, but I am the boss and as far as yesterday is concerned, it's water over the dam. There I stood, as Jeb

Stuart did, ready to unbuckle my sword, but business went on as usual.

I met a great group of folks in and around Fort Leavenworth, the Mayor and other prominent citizens. I played golf on Wednesdays when all of the City of Leavenworth professional people were off, doctors, lawyers, and car salesmen. Sometimes we would play in one group, maybe ten or twelve. When that many balls are on the green it appears that it has snowed. It was great fun, everyone had bets with others.

I made friends with a lot officers who went places from Leavenworth College. Some went on to the War College and became Generals. One friend in particular, whom I had served with in the Canal Zone, went from the college to the Pentagon and became a Colonel. He was the father of my son's friend Peter, who is now the Chief of Staff of the Army. Whenever I needed a favor, I would call Colonel Schoomaker, he could do wonders. He also has a son who is a Brigadier General in the Army at Fort Detrick, MD. This General Schoomaker is on the list for two stars and did a great deal for me years ago when he was at Walter Reed. It sure was good to have friends in high places.

The former Captain Middlestadt, whom I had gone to school with at Fort Benning, became a student there in 1959. It was great seeing him again, we played golf and had a beer or two when we could. He had a nice family also.

In 1960, General McGarr received orders for Vietnam. He was also promoted to Three Star General. He asked me to go with him and denying his request turned out to be my biggest mistake ever. It would only have been for a couple of years and I would have received another promotion. I was talked out of it by my wife as she convinced me that the boys needed me around. I should have sent her home to New Jersey and went, it all would have worked out.

I am sure that some of you reading this story wonder how I fell into such a glamorous life. When I worked for these Generals, from Bradley down the line, I did my best. I will brag about myself when I compare myself with others that I served with, don't get me wrong, I served over, with, and under a hell of a lot of good men. Take General McGarr for instance, he was a West Pointer and could have had any West Point Officer he wanted as an aide, yet he chose me. I often think of this, but I built up a close relationship with him that allowed him to devote all of his time to doing his job, I did the rest. I anticipated his wishes, took care of every detail, and he relied on me to do that. I was his right arm and believe that had I gone to Vietnam with him, he would not have had the stress causing a heart condition that sent him back to the States early. He and his wife told me several times, "George," we don't know what we would do without you." However, I do know, as close as we were, that I did many things that he would not have asked a West Point Lieutenant or Captain to do. Some of the chores were personal, and other unofficial. It's hard to explain, but if General McGarr wanted a project researched or accomplished, and did not want to get involved, I was his taskmaster. I liked these operations knowing that he knew I would realize the course of action to be taken without any recourse. With this type of personal relationship, he and I became very close, almost thinking alike.

I stayed at Fort Leavenworth and got myself assigned to the Army prison there. At first I was the Executive Officer of the Guard Company along with another Captain, then took over as athletic director of the prison. This was a real challenge. We had intramural baseball, football, boxing, softball, ping pong, the entire works. Scheduling was a real chore, but I had several enlisted men to help.

It was interesting to watch prisoners play sports against each other. They were really tough, especially in boxing and football. We would let them go at it really good as it was a good way for them to work off steam. In addition to being athletic director, I was also a corrections officer. I sat on parole boards, tutored in classes, and supervised the farm. The prisoners worked the farm and raised animals. We had hens for eggs, which were sold to the residents of Fort Leavenworth, ran a beautiful green house, and always had flowers for all occasions.

There was one prisoner who was in for murder and was sentenced to death by hanging. It so happened that I was the duty officer the night this was to happen. A Stay of Execution was attempted that night, but denied. At twelve midnight, the Chaplain, the Commandant of the prison, eight honorary pall bearers, and myself went to his cell. He had his last meal request given to him earlier. The Chaplain had a few words with him and we marched him out to the gallows. The first Sergeant of the Guard Company and another sergeant were on the gallows with him. He was placed over the trap door, then a hood was put over his head and a rope was placed around his neck with a block of wood inside of the rope. The Chaplain was praying as all of the above was performed in a few seconds. With all in place the door was sprung open and the young man fell several feet with his arms tied behind him and his legs bound. At the end of the fall he pulled his legs up bending his knees for a few seconds, he then urinated which ran down off his shoes. Twenty three minutes later he was pronounced dead, cut loose, put in an ambulance, and carried away to be buried in Potters Field.

Another interesting point I wish to mention, remember I sat on a general court martial back in Washington in 1957, the victim that was sentenced to Leavenworth prison was still there and was the librarian, we had several discussions together.

As athletic director, I formed a basketball team of all trustees and was allowed to go play at the local colleges in the area, we were pretty good too. I had one tall black dude who would dunk really good, the team was built around him.

Another time I had the football team practicing and was showing the quarterback how to faint back and throw. This was only practice and no one was to hit hard, but as I fainted talking to my quarterback another prisoner from the opposing team came around and gave me a blind side clip. My left knee made a noise like a pistol shot. A few months later I had to go to the Hospital in Denver, Colorado to have this knee operated on. To this day, it still hurts and I have a thirty percent disability from the Veterans Administration.

I had been at Fort Leavenworth for almost four years now, it had been great for the twins, one place for four years. Leavenworth was a great place for kids, the Fort had everything, including a golf course, theater, and bowling alley. One did not have to leave the Fort for anything.

The Army had a regulation that when a non regular officer completed ten years of commissioned service, with over twenty years total service, he must retire. On 1 June 1962 I left the service, I had a great tour of service. I met many fine people, Truman, Bradley, Eisenhower, Nixon, and many more. I had served in two conflicts, walked up the Bank in Normandy, crossed the Elbe River, and met the Russians. I had ridden down Pennsylvania Avenue on horseback, had worked at the White House, met Cardinal Spellman, and stayed at the Waldorf Astoria and Blair House.

The medals that I earned for my twenty four years of service included the Good Conduct Medal with four knots for more than twelve years enlisted service, The Combat Infantry Badge with star for combat service in Europe and one campaign in Korea, The Bronze Star Medal with two oak leaf clusters, The Army Commendation Medal with four oak leaf clusters, The European Theatre of Operation with five campaign stars, the Korean Theatre with one star, and other service medals that went with this period.

I was sired by a man who only traveled to two states and District of Columbia, yet I've traveled to twenty five countries, plus almost every state in the union.

I am so proud of my service to my country and, "Once a soldier, always a soldier" to my dying day.

At this time I was only forty-two years of age and really felt naked. With more than twenty-four years of service, I was released with no fan fare, no parade, no handshake, just here are your retirement papers.

George's "cabbage patch"

Still loves horses

My Grandson, Jonathan, age 19 at Rutgers University.

George & Violet Together since 1972

Receiving Member Guest
Trophy, 1979

"Gran-paw" and J.W. at
seventh tee, Ft.
Monmouth, 2002

257

CIVILIAN LIFE AGAIN

I had purchased a 1959 Pontiac, and after loading our furniture for shipment to Alexandria, Virginia, I loaded my wife and two sons into my car and headed East via Canada. We arrived in New Jersey about a week later. After a short visit with Kitty's parents we headed to Waples Mill, Virginia. My sister Lucy had bought the old home place so we moved in with her pending further decisions. With my experience as a corrections officer back at the Leavenworth Prison, I landed a job with the Fairfax County Sheriffs Department in a few days. This wasn't really my cup of tea. A few weeks later Kitty's father called to say we could have the old frame duplex house in West Palm Beach, Florida. After talking this over with my wife we decided to travel to Florida and look at the house. Remember, back when I had worked for General Bradley, we visited Kitty's parents at that house.

We arrived there in July at a time when the weather was hot, and moved into a motel with a swimming pool for the boys. After examining the house we decided not to take her father's gift, maybe another mistake, I don't know. However, we did return to New Jersey and moved in with my in-laws for a week or so. We went house hunting and found one for rent in Eatontown, New Jersey. I moved in before school started so the boys attended Monmouth Regional in Tinton Falls. I joined the golf club at Fort Monmouth, the boys started school, and Kitty went back to nursing.

One day when I was playing golf in August of 1962, I met a gentleman who worked for John Hancock Insurance Company. When I informed him that I had recently retired from the Army he asked if I wanted a position with his company selling insurance. Needing a job, I immediately took him up on his offer. His name was Tom Davis, a real Irish man, who took me under his wing and taught me the trade. He being in a managerial position worked with me for several months, and then I went on my own doing fairly well. In fact, during the year of 1963, was the first time that I had ever made over ten thousand dollars in one year, selling insurance was OK. I did good and was offered an assistant manager's job after I finished an insurance school, but would have to move to Baltimore. During the summer 1964, I resigned from John Hancock.

After the boys spent one year at Monmouth Regional we decided to send them to Stanton Military Academy in Virginia the last two years. They went there as juniors, but it took them three years to graduate. After graduation, one went to York College in Pennsylvania, and the other to a Junior College in Maryland. This is the first time they had ever been apart.

The following year my father-in-law passed on. My wife wanting to be closer to her mother caused us to move to Farmingdale, New Jersey. I had bought a Chevrolet from a dealership in Farmingdale that was owned by George Matthews, but was operated by his daughter and son-in-law, Vera and Alex Vince. My wife had gone to school with Vera so we became close friends. One day when I stopped by the garage, Vera asked me if I wanted a job as service manager of the dealership. I had never been a mechanic, but I had been a maintenance officer in the Army and had been to a management school. I took the job and moved into a house directly behind the dealership. I had to walk about one hundred feet to work. This was my second real civilian job. I had to get up and go to work, sometimes one of the mechanics would remind me that I wasn't in the Army anymore.

I remained as service manager until 1972 when Mr. Mathews sold the dealership. Vera's husband, Al and I became friends and played a lot of golf together. He belonged to Manasquan River, a beautiful club. He had me there as his guest and I invited him to Fort Monmouth. We won his member guest one year, and again in 1979 at Fort Monmouth. The Bristol, as they called their member guest, was in those days second to none. What a show they put on. I also won a set of Wilson Staff clubs there when Al took a chance on them for me.

I made many friends during my tenure at Matthew's Chevrolet. I joined the local Kawanis Club and became a good citizen of the community. This was Kitty's hometown, she knew all of the old timers even though she had been away for twenty years or so.

I joined the Methodist church, and it wasn't long before I was an officer of the church, new blood had landed. I told my wife many times over the years that as soon as the twins were gone that I was going also, she couldn't believe it. My sister Frances also would tell Kitty that if she didn't stop nagging me one day I would leave. This was always in my mind, but felt that I must stay until the twins were gone.

Grant had finished two years at York College and joined the Army to become a helicopter pilot. Gary finished his two years of college and went to x-ray school in Red Bank, New Jersey. Upon completion he took a job in the hospital of Culpepper, Virginia. Before Gary left he married a nurse from Marlboro, New Jersey who was a nurse in Red Bank. Before he left for Culpepper I gave him a nice wedding with the reception at Fort Monmouth Officers Club, Grant was his best man. He got married on a Saturday and departed Sunday for Virginia. Grant reported back to his Army base in Texas.

It was that same Sunday that I took my razor and tooth brush and left also. My wife was reading the Sunday paper when I came downstairs and asked me where I was going, I reminded her of my previous plans, that I too was leaving, she was stunned.

In 1970, as service manager, I met a very nice divorcee from Freehold. I saw her once in awhile when her car needed service.

After leaving my home that Sunday morning I proceeded to find an apartment near Fort Monmouth. I also called my friend from Freehold and told her what I had done. She was shocked, but I believe pleasantly so. We had dinner that very Sunday evening with her telling me that while I was seeking an apartment that she had plenty of room and that I could stay with her for a few days. I never left, and we were married two years later. When I was a young boy my father warned his children never to trust a Jew, black person, or a Catholic. Here I had just married a Catholic lady, had gotten married by Seymour Burke, Mayor of Farmingdale, and one of my guests, a black man. As I thanked everyone for coming, I told the story about my father's feelings on certain people saying I am sure he has just turned over in his grave. This created a roar.

As I was out of a job with the Chevrolet Dealership sold, I applied for Unemployment. Here I was, no sons, no wife, no job, the same man that had done so much over the last thirty four years. I left with twelve dollars in my pocket and a small TV set. Vera and Al had given me a car as severance pay, and I gave everything else including a new car to Kitty.

I had left Kitty with all our furniture, everything, plus about ten thousands dollars. I then immediately closed our checking account failing to tell her that I had done so. She wrote a check for the full amount with the check bouncing. I then had to cover the check. Kitty also soon found out where I was living and visited one evening. I have an ankle that cracks when I walk up a stairway for some reason. When she rang the doorbell, Violet peaked through the curtain and signaled me that it was Kitty. I started up the stairway with my ankle making a cracking noise, and Kitty yelled out, "I know you're there George, I can hear your ankle." It seems that she had learned one thing about me over the last thirty years. She told all of our mutual friends of this visit and hearing the ankle noise. My friends later when seeing me would ask, "How is your ankle George?" Very funny.

Kitty, the mother of my twins may have had a few bad traits, but none worth expanding on. In general, she was a fine lady, basically a religious person who believed in God. A great mother, good cook, and outstanding housekeeper. She was an above-average nurse, but a hypochondriac. I believe there were many good attributes. She stood by me in thick and thin and did her best. We just moved apart, and she deserved more than I gave her. May the wind always blow at her back in her remaining years.

After six month's vacation I took a job with a trucking company which in a couple of years became a bore, plus the commute was about twenty-five miles. I took another vacation, mowed the lawn, and played golf.

Needing to go back to work, I took a job as service manager of a new car dealership in Red Bank. I did good and made the best money of my life. I also won a trip to Las Vegas, so my new wife Violet and I flew there for a week's vacation.

Some time passed when one day I read that the Cadillac Agency in Red Bank was looking for some new blood in

their service department. I went to see the ov
job. Two years later this dealership was sold
work again. More golf, flowers, and mowing

While working at the Cadillac Agency one of my
customers became the second best friend I've ever had. He
had two Cadillac Sedan Broughams, one for himself and one
for his wife. After several visits we got to know each other
better, discovering that we only lived two blocks apart. This
worked out fine as he never had to bring his cars in to the
dealership. I would pick them up on my way in to work.
This gentlemen, Philip Brokstein, known to most as "Brock"
works for the Florsheim Shoe Company. I would help him
with his other chores also, fix the fence, take care of the
lawn, and chauffeur him if he needed a ride to the airport. I
have come to love this man, he is like a brother. Our
birthdays are in February and we celebrate by going to a
great lobster house in Newark, Don Pepe's. Last year Violet
and I split a seven pound lobster, what a feast we had. There
is nothing he and I wouldn't do for each other.

One day while playing golf with Alex Vince, my old boss
at Matthews Chevrolet in Manasquan, one of our opponents
was the owner of Park Chevrolet in Neptune, New Jersey.
Upon learning that I had experience in auto service
departments, this gentlemen, George Van Wickle, hired me
to help operate his service department. I remained there until
1985, and in the spring of that year I caught a real bad cold,
plus I was experiencing, as the doctor described, TIA's. I
would get dizzy, left arm numb, and lose my speech. Upon
examination I was told to take some time off, which I did,
retiring for the second time in my life, more golf, but no grass
cutting.

My new friend Violet and her former husband had
purchased a colonial type, four bedroom home near Freehold,

Jersey. When he left her she was awarded child ɹpport, but he got away with murder on the amount. At the time I met Violet, she was having a difficult time making ends meet, and I only had my Army retirement so back to work I went as I too had to pay alimony to my first wife. Vi and her first husband owned the house jointly, but in a few years together we saved enough money to buy her first husband's interest in the home from him. As I recall, we paid eighteen thousand five hundred dollars to him. I had to borrow about eight thousand to meet this demand. In a few years with me working and hustling, I paid this loan off.

The lady I had just married had been deserted by the father of her six children, and I had just jumped from the frying pan into the fire, what had I done. My golfing friends were stunned. Here I had just left my first wife for nagging me, and now I married a gal with six kids, well only five, one was gone. Those kids could eat two loaves of bread from french toast, two pounds of bacon, tons of cereal, it was a good thing that I could shop at the Fort Monmouth commissary. Lots of things happened in the next fifteen years with me raising those children. As the children graduated from high school, they had a choice of going to college or going out on their own. Like my original early years, as each child got old enough, they split, as the term goes, leaving Vi and me alone in a four-bedroom house. I can look back now and say, I done good. One guy finished college and is a teacher. He is married now and has twins. They are scattered all over the county doing their thing. It wasn't an easy task, some grief, but generally happiness. I served my purgatory, and in my opinion deserve my days on the links smelling the roses.

In July 1984, Violet and I being alone in a four room colonial home, decided to sell. We bought a townhouse across the street from the Fort Monmouth Golf Course, very convenient. Upon moving in we met a nice young couple, and the man had a job with a company that fused railroad tracks together. That company would hold their annual meeting at the Greenbrier Resort near Lewisburg, West Virginia, where my son, Gary lives on Muddy Creek Mountain. This young railroad man, Jerry Hines, and I became close friends, and once as he told me that he was heading for the Greenbrier for the meeting and to play golf, I asked him to leave a cart and green fee receipt paid in full charging it to his company with the pro for me as I was soon going to Lewisburg to visit my son. This he did, so I got to play the Greenbrier all day playing the old white and new course. It was great fun. When one plays there they are in high cotton. Now my grandson who attends Lewisburg High School plays some of their matches there. He tells me, hey pop, I played at the Greenbrier and I earned it the hard way.

After I recovered from these health problems and took off for about a year, I took a part-time job driving a school bus for the Monmouth Regional bus system. I only drove for class trips and sporting events. I worked only when I wanted to as the dispatcher and I got along great. I arranged to drive all golf trips so I could play also, doing so most of the times with the respective coaches. I played a lot of nice courses that I normally would not have gotten to play in the area. Took some nice trips to Philadelphia, New York City, the Meadowlands for pro games, Delaware Water Gap, and along the Coast of New Jersey. I even helped coach the golf team from Manalapan High School, as their coach did not play golf so knew nothing of the game. The athletic director furnished me a jacket and cap, that was nice. This went on for almost five years.

During the year 1990, I started getting chest pains. I went through all sorts of tests at Walter Reed and was told of my problem. I had an artery ninety percent closed, and that angioplasty would help. This was done immediately at Deborah Hospital here in New Jersey. Since then, I've gone to Deborah, the greatest of all heart and lung hospitals, for two more angiograms finding that the original operation was still holding up. I also have as my heart doctor, one of the best, Doctor John Checton, who has an office in Long Branch. He looks after me like I am his father. Off and on, if I exercise too much, I may feel some pain. I take medication and most of the time I feel great.

As my son Grant had just been promoted to Lieutenant Colonel, his twin brother and I pinned his silver leafs on his shoulders, another very proud moment in my life.

As for the twin sons, Grant was released from the Army after a few years and went back to York College and got his bachelors degree. He floundered for a while from one job to another, and then went back to school and became a nurse. After he graduated as a nurse and was working in a hospital in the Washington area, he met a patient whom he fell in love with and married. A few years later she developed cancer and died. During this period he went back to school and got his masters degree in psychology, he also upon graduating from nursing, got a reserve commission in the Army Nurse Corp. Today he is a Lieutenant Colonel and working at the health clinic at Quantico Marine Base in Virginia.

For Gary, after marriage he became an x-ray technician. He was having trouble in one knee that was damaged back at Fort Leavenworth junior high. After three bad operations the knee was fused. He became more crippled as time went on. The leg began to get shorter requiring lifts on that shoe. He is in constant pain as his rib cage and spine are out of line. As he could not stand for any period of time he had to go on social security. Needing something to do he attended a seminary in Kentucky and became an Episcopal Deacon being ordained in Charleston, West Virginia. He is a retired preacher around the area of Lewisburg, West Virginia. He either assists or conducts services in small churches in that area, some congregations being as small as eight or ten. For this there is no salary, just mileage. Lucky for him that he remarried another nurse after his first wife divorced him, who is one of the head nurses in the Lewisburg Hospital. A son was born to them in 1981, and is my only blood grandson. He is my buddy and we love each other dearly. He is a good golfer who spent the summer of 1996 with me in New Jersey. Back at his home, which is on top of Muddy Creek Mountain, he has nothing to do. I am looking forward to him coming back for the 1997 golf season here in New Jersey.

267

This year he will have a paying job where he will be saving for college.

I have mentioned brother Raymond earlier and how he was my best friend ever. During the 1950's he was fortunate in becoming partners with two wealthy investors who bought some acreage in Fairfax County near the courthouse, and propositioned Raymond that if he did all of the work in building a mobile home estate park they would furnish the money and make him a partner. Raymond completed this task in a year or so constructing three hundred and fifty concrete slabs with sewage, electric, the entire program. As a section was finished people moved in. About ten years later the park was sold, and when all was settled brother Raymond took home about one million or so.

Raymond bought an old farm in Jeffersonton, Virginia, rebuilt the home, took up golf, sent his daughters to college, and use to call me to come on down either to play golf at his club or go south with a group from his club. He would tell me, "George, you get this far and I'll take care of the rest."

Ray belonged to the Fauquier Springs Country Club located between Warranton and Culpepper. Before the member-guest tournament there would be a Calcutta, that is when one can buy a team through a bidding process. Some teams would go for four or five hundred. Ray would keep bidding until he had who he wanted. We won the tournament one year, it was medal play with handicap. On Saturday he shot a seventy-four and I followed up on Sunday with a seventy-five. We immediately got a sand bagger reputation. Lots of times we played alone just enjoying each other's company. We would play "look-backs" for a buck or two.

268

"Two country boys." Waple with brother and good friend Raymond.

I soon learned never to tell Ray that we needed his putt, he would yell back at me stating, "Don't you think I don't know that." I would tuck my tail between my legs and walk away.

On the ninth hole which was on a slope of about thirty degrees I had about a two-foot putt. We had just been pressed for forty five dollars on the tee and the putt was going to break at least a foot, I was nervous as hell without him telling me, in violation of his own rule, boy, you had better make that putt or you will walk back to Jersey. After looking at this putt, lining it up from all directions, I gave it my best stroke. My ball ended up twenty five feet down the hill off the green, ninety dollars down the drain. Back in the club house our opponents consoled me saying, "That's OK George, we will buy you a beer." Ray wasn't speaking, but when he did speak he told me that I should have gotten the first putt closer.

Brother Ray was a lover of hard-shell crabs. He would call me knowing that Vi and I also liked them. Once we met in Maryland at Saturday noon and proceeded to Pope's Creek, a tin shanty on the Potomac River where crabs came in all sizes. The tables were bare, but covered with brown paper. Ray would order two or three dozen of the larger ones backed up with several pitchers of beer. On this particular trip, his son, Hugh and wife, came along, we ate crabs for several hours. My wife could devour a dozen easily. From this establishment we moved on to another nice place for dinner. Sunday noon we had another feast of crabs before heading home. There were times when Ray would have us down to his farm for a crab feast that he would prepare, he was a hell of a man.

One time the pro from his club arranged that we go to Saw Grass, near Jacksonville, Florida, and we rented condos right on the course. At night some read, some watched TV, but there were about eight of the group that played hearts. One evening the pro got so excited that he jumped out of his chair and grabbed the chandelier to swing on like a monkey and pulled it out of the ceiling. About a month after I returned home, I received a note from him asking for a donation to cover my part of the damage. I never answered his letter. One evening during this same trip, brother Ray and I decided to buy a couple of steaks and eat in. While my steak was cooking I realized I had forgotten something to go with our meal, when I returned from the store my steak was gone, boy was I pissed. To this day when I stop by his club one of those chaps will call out to me, "George, how was that steak?"

Ray was over fifty when he took up golf, but was a natural. He and I won a few bucks, we always teamed up. We won the club member guest one year going away.

One year I went down on a Friday as the group was leaving on Saturday. Ray had arranged a game for 10 a.m. Friday morning, so I left New Jersey about four a.m., and we played a whipsaw fivesome. We both shot a seventy-five; what fun we had together. I won enough to pay for my trip without hitting Ray up. Violet and I would go down as she loved that old remodeled farm house.

I had another brother Rufus living in Florida at this time. At one time Ray called and asked if I wanted to visit Rufus, off I went. We stopped and played golf every time we saw a sign, Golf Course. In Columbia, South Carolina, we pulled into the Columbia County Course even though the signs on entrance stated "Private, members only." We introduced ourselves to the pro and asked to play. The pro pointed out that the club was private, only members and their guest could play. At this point, Ray said, "Is the place for sale?" This statement really cracked up a man standing close by. With this he told us that he was alone, getting ready to play and that we could be his guest. On the first tee I noticed this gentlemen to be left handed as am I. After introductions we discovered that our host was the Methodist bishop of South Carolina. No money was bet, but I laid a couple of stain glass windows on him, he came back on the next hole with a couple of pews. We had fun and later headed on down the road.

There was a bond between my brother Ray and me that was outstanding. From the time that I was knee high to a grasshopper, he not only was a brother, he was a buddy, a pal, and a friend. Even in his alcoholic days we stuck together. Of course, after I went into the Army, we were apart for many years. These years were tough ones for him and his family. Margaret, his wife, lived through hell having their children, moving constantly, but Maggie was always

271

there for him. After the war Ray became the great person that he was cut out to be. During those years our bond started to cement again. Up until his death what great times we had together, he was everything to me. I sure loved that man and miss him dearly. I know when we met again, he will tell me, I know we need this putt.

My big brother, my friend, Ray, passed on in the late eighties. His wife, the same little girl that had her first child on a cold January night in 1933 lives on. Four hundred acres of the farm were sold off before Ray died, but he kept fifty acres, and built a beautiful brick home there. One can look West and when the sun goes behind the Blue Ridge Mountains there is nothing but beauty. Ray named this home, his last, "The Trails End." Ray and Maggie had six wonderful children, a close-knit group and looked after their Mama, a charming lady whom I consider a sister. I visit her whenever I can.

At this writing I have only one sister left out of a family of eight, four boys and four girls. I tell Lucy, look, once we had two foursomes and now we are a twosome, don't leave me, it's no fun playing a single. When I first told her this, she not being a golfer, did not understand, when I explained, she said, "Oh, now I get it."

Over the years my legal counsel has been a country lawyer named Alex Luvchuk from Freehold. He represented my new wife over the years in her divorce proceedings and other required dealings such as a house closing and the like. I became to know this gentlemen quite well over the years, and now he is my favorite person. He is almost as country as I am. The best thing about him is his fees are reasonable, and he pays for lunch. Also renders a lot of legal information on the cuff. I do some investigating for him and serve most of his summonses.

To sum up my golf exploits over the past forty-five years, I can state that I have had seven holes in ones. I won the Monmouth County New Jersey Seniors at the age of sixty five at Hominy Hill County Golf Course, shooting a seventy seven. I won the Class "A" Flight at Fort Monmouth, New Jersey in 1990, and won the Eighty-Third Division Reunion Tournament twice. Of course most of my opponents were old like me. My lowest handicap ever was an eight at Fort Monmouth one summer a few years back. Not bad for a Country Boy who never had a formal lesson. Another chap, Tom Pugh, Lieutenant Colonel retired, and I won five member - member tournaments at Fort Monmouth.

Much to my sorrow is that I did not attend all of the 83rd Infantry Division Association Reunions, but some were impossible due to active duty requirements. After release from the Army in 1962, however, I could have attended some. I have no excuse except of my obligation to the twins and shortage of capital. After I left my first wife and took up with my second wife, Vi, who had five children, money for travel, hotels, etc., was not plentiful. It was not until 1990 that I became active in the Association. At the Memorial Ceremonies I soon discovered that they were being conducted in a haphazard fashion. There would be a grouping, but with no formal formation. People, my comrades, would just gather for the memorial service.

After my second reunion I talked with my good friend Fred Barnes, telling him I can do this better. I suggested to a former Captain Macaluco (now deceased), a Company Commander of "G" Company, that if we were going to have a parade, let's do it right. He agreed. Instead of a grouping of veterans, let us form in a military fashion and if we were to march let's do it according to the manual. At first I think my buddies resented my motivation, but soon became thrilled

273

**Captain G.H. Waple, Retired, leading 83rd Infantry Division to
memorial service September 1994.**

at the idea. They liked to act like soldiers again, be called to
attention, and march in cadence to my command, I loved it
also. I was a combat veteran conducting a service that I had
for years became accustomed to. After several years, now
Colonel Macaluco, told me, "George, you're in charge." One
of the biggest thrills of my life was when I formed all of the
attendees who wished to march into three companies,
representing the entire 83rd Division, and called them to
attention by commanding, "Division attention, right face,
forward, march." I had gone from a First Sergeant to
Division Commander. My comrades responded well,
standing tall and marching in step to the beat of the Division
band. I do not perform as a former captain, but as a former
First Sergeant. I really get a kick out of having my comrades

tell me after our memorial service, "Hey, top dog, you done good."

My congratulation goes out to former Captain Macaluco of "George" Company for the job he has done during these reunions, he is, I think, the only company Commander left and I believe I am the only original First Sergeant of the 331st Infantry left, also being an original member of the Division Association formed at Fort Myer, Virginia, by Brig. General Ferenbaugh, the Assistant Division Commander after W.W.II.

Three of us, one being from original Cadre like me and Fred Barnes, keep in close touch. Barnes or I call each other several times a month, he has a laugh that I love.

During the early nineties, the Fairfax School Board decided that an elementary school was needed in the Waple's Mill area (kindergarten through sixth grade). After much discussion, the Board finally decided the name of the school would be "Waple's Mill Elementary School." The land for the school was originally called "Waple Land," which made the name even more appropriate.

The school was to be dedicated May 1992 and I was invited to be one of the guest speakers. How proud I was. Even though I now lived in New Jersey, I was next in line of the Waples to represent the Waple family.

I immediately had a portrait of my Great Grandfather which I presented to the school at the dedication.

There were thirteen Waple offspring at the dedication. One asked me to take a seat with the Waples, not knowing that I was supposed to sit on the stage and be a speaker; she thought I was being too forward.

When I was introduced and gave my talk, all of my relatives were shocked. I had prepared thoroughly and knew exactly what I was doing. Upon finishing my talk, I then presented the portrait of my Great Grandfather to the Principal of the school. I received a large ovation from the sixth grade, teachers, staff, faculty, but most importantly, my family. I am sure Papa and Mama were looking down on me saying, "George Henry, you done good." The school hung their portrait in the Library.

After each talk my wife attended, she always criticized me for saying that I was a high school drop out — this really upset her.

It was around 2002 that she wrote the Commonwealth of Virginia Board of Education asking that they would give her husband a High School Diploma as he had accomplished much more education than high school over the years going to military and other civilian schools.

I then received a letter from Daniel A. Domenech, the superintendent of Fairfax County school system, telling me that during my visit to the Waples Mill Elementary School, May 24, 2002, they would present my high school diploma to me.

Waples Mill Elementary Receives Official Blessing

" **A** nd the county official hammered in the stake and called it a school."

So pronounced sixth grader Jenn-Claire Kinchen during her

by Eric Peters

speech at dedication ceremonies held on Monday for Waples Mill Elementary School in Oakton.

Waples Mill is the newest elementary school in Fairfax County, and has been in operation since last September.

The entire student body of 560 pre-schoolers through sixth graders gathered to hear Superintendent Robert R. Spillane, Area III Superintendent Murriel F. Price, a host of local dignitaries and a member of the Waples family discuss the history behind the new school and talk about the importance of education.

George Henry Waple (right) presents a painting of the first George Henry Waple to Waples Mill Elementary School principal Cabell W. Lloyd.

Waples Mill principal Cabell W. Lloyd began by dedicating the school to the children. "They represent the reason why we're all here this morning," he said.

Spillane praised the hard work and commitment of the school board, parents and citizenry to their public education system.

He pointed to the $500 million in bond issues voters have approved over the last seven years that have been used to build 14 new schools, including Waples Mill, and renovate several existing ones.

"A lot of good people have seen to it that this has been accomplished," he said.

Area III Superintendent Murriel F. Price dedicated Waples Mill to "all the young people here in the audience today, and to all the future generations of young people who will come here to learn."

"It is my great hope that some of you will become leaders not only in Fairfax County, but in the nation as well," he continued. "We may even have a young president with us here

today."

Sixth grader Beau Morgan gave a speech about the history of the Waples Mill area. He described how the name is derived from the presence of the mill nearby, which was built in the early part of the 19th century by George Henry Waple, who emigrated from Ireland in 1814.

"I guess you'd have to call him the first," said his namesake, George Henry Waple, who also spoke during the ceremonies.

"We are very proud of our roots," he said.

Waple, who was one of the 11 members of his family present for the dedication, later presented a painting of his ancestor to the principal.

The portrait of the original George Henry Waple will be displayed within the school to honor and protect the memory of the history behind the school's name, according to Lloyd.

"I'd like to thank everyone involved in the school system," Waples said. He concluded with these remarks which he directed at the students: "Stay in school, study hard, obey your teachers and your parents."

277

On the wall behind the stage, drawings children of the elementary school hung.

Presenting photo to Mr. Brooks, principal of Waples Mill Elementary School. After giving talk to sixth graders telling of my life at Waples Mill.

What a show the school put on. Washington 10 o'clock News, Channel 5 was there and many of my friends and family. I was bursting with pride as well as Violet, my wife. After the ceremony, there was a reception including the sixth-grade class, friends, family and the entire staff and faculty.

As a result of the TV coverage, I received calls and letters telling me they had seen me on the 10 o'clock news in Washington and congratulating me. I am a member of the Battle of the Bulge organization at Fort Monmouth, New Jersey, consisting of the group of veterans who served in WWII and fought in that battle. I think we have seventy or so members. There is also a national association of which I am a member. Several years ago we installed a monument on the Fort and have had it landscaped beautifully. Each Memorial Day, Veteran's Day, and Christmas, I place a wreath at the monument. The wreaths were designed by my wife and are beautiful.

George and Violet, placing a Christmas wreath at the monument in remembrance of the Bulge and the veterans who fought there.

Around the turn of the century in the year 2000, I got a brainstorm that I would have an eightieth birthday party, which would be held at the Fort Monmouth Officers Club. I made a list of all relatives and friends I could think of bringing the list to eighty-one people. My wife thought I was nuts. The invitations were sent out, arrangements for a band, red carpet requested, and a dinner menu of steak, fish and chicken to be served. The party was a great success: my two sons and grandson from West Virginia and Virginia in attendance. I invited all of my golfing buddies, neighbors, doctors, lawyers and to get up to eighty people I must have invited, the garbage collector, too. Of the eighty folks I invited, eighty showed up. What a party!

George and Violet at 80th birthday party

Jonathan Waple, 20, walks down red carpet with his grandmother.

As a result of many WWII, Korea, and unrelated war stories, I discussed my life with many people.

This brought questions and inquires about talking to local civic organizations, schools and military groups such as the VFW, American Legion, and gatherings of active duty soldiers. My first such talk was an invite of a Vincent Sutphin, a charter member of the Fairfax County VFW. Vincent had been an old school mate and neighbor nearby Waples Mill. I set a date, gathered most of my material and set out for Fairfax. After WWII, Vincent had contacted me at

Fort Myer, Virginia, and asked me to visit one of the meetings and tell my old friends of the parts I'd played in the War and asked if I'd like to join the VFW, becoming a charter member. I liked the idea and did join, attending every monthly meeting thereafter. In a year or so, I kind of forgot the chapter and failed to attend, but I was still a charter member. This was brought up at the meeting and my talk thereafter. Well, I knocked them dead with my stories and experiences. This was the beginning of my talk engagements.

About two-thirds of these talks I got local news coverage.

These talks were a great experience and I got better and better with each talk.

Being interviewed by Channel 12 News on May 24, 2003

As the word spread, a retired colonel and assistant professor of Brookdale Community College heard of me and asked if I would like to join a committee he was starting called Center for WWII Studies and Conflict Resolution. This proved to become another great experience, especially when I would think that I was just a country boy from Waples Mill.

Because of my news articles, I was invited to attend a New Jersey TV show for an interview. I was thrilled and did so; the interview only lasted twelve minutes, but was replayed eight or ten times during the morning telecast – I called all friends and asked them to watch.

The New Jersey Museum at Sea Girt also did a documentary on my experiences in Korea.

Brookdale Community College also taped a show where I was being interviewed by Colonel Zigo, the history professor I spoke of before. This documentary has continued to be shown on the Brookdale Channel almost weekly.

Being taped for a documentary of my Korean Seminar at the Sea Girt Museum.

Being honored by Colts Neck High School

I spoke at Monmouth County, Middletown, Red Bank libraries, the Colts Neck Women's Club and the Red Bank Senior Citizen Home. At the beginning of this talk, there were about seventy-five attendees, at half time, only about one-half were awake, not that my speech was boring, but it was nap time to them.

Demonstrating the wearing of my first campaign hat that I wore as a member of the Third Horse Cavalry to the entire student body at the Shrewsbury Elementary School in New Jersey. I told them either my head got bigger or the hat had gotten smaller.

News Transcript

Serving Colts Neck, Englishtown Freehold, Manalapan, Marlboro

February 26, 2003   Volume 115, Number 8   www.gmnews.com   50¢

Soldier's story is firsthand account of Army life, death

Ret. Capt. George Waple recounts experiences for high school ROTC class

BY DAVE BENJAMIN
Staff Writer

Before learning how to deal with the future, students in the Freehold Regional High School District's Junior ROTC program at Colts Neck High School learned firsthand from a retired army captain what it was like to be involved in World War II.

George H. Waple III

Lt. Col. Jim Stayer, senior naval science instructor, introduced Capt. George H. Waple III, 82, of Eatontown and told his students that Waple "can be described as a walking history book."

Waple then spoke with the students about his 24 years of service to the nation.

In the spring of 1944, Waple, then a first sergeant in the 83rd Infantry Division, shipped out of New York City on the *USS George Washington* to arrive shortly in Liverpool, England. Only a few weeks later, his division landed on Omaha Beach shortly after D-Day, relieving the 101st Airborne Division near Carenton, France.

Waple introduced the students to what was known as Operation Overlord.

"In 1942 and 1943, we were fighting the Germans in Africa, but President (Franklin Delano) Roosevelt and U.S. Chief of Staff Gen. (George) Marshall, (along with) Gen. (Dwight) Eisenhower, Gen. (Omar) Bradley and Gen. (Bernard) Montgomery, decided we had to have an operation going across from England to France," said Waple. "Before we made the invasion of France, Bradley made the first blunder of the operation."

Waple told the students that Bradley and his staff loaded troops on landing ship tanks and made a mock invasion near Southampton, England. German U-boats were tipped off about the practice invasion and the Allies lost 700 men.

Using maps, Waple described the routes taken by the 101st and 82nd Airborne Divisions as they flew into Normandy, France.

"They didn't go straight across (the English Channel), they went around (to get to the target area)," said Waple. "It was a disaster because the Germans heard that they were gong to glide into that area. The Germans (were prepared and they) killed a lot of men."

He explained that more than 700 ships, 4,000 landing craft and 176,000 troops were involved in the D-Day landing operation on June 6, 1944, including American, British, Canadian, New Zealand, free Polish and free French troops, as well as other Allies. The British landed at Sword Beach and Gold Beach, while the Canadians landed at June Beach.

Coming across the English Channel were American troops of the 1st Division, the 29th Division and the 4th Division, Waple said.

"They landed at Omaha and Utah beaches and the British landed over here (pointing to Sword Beach on the map)," said Waple. "We made it, but there were a lot of people killed."

Statistics provided by Martin K.A. Morgan, research historian, National D-Day Museum, New Orleans, La., indicate there were 6,603 American casualties during that invasion, including 1,465 killed in action; 1,928 missing in action and presumed dead; 3,184 wounded in action; and 26 taken as prisoners of war.

"I was a sergeant at the time," Waple told the teens. "My unit was still in England, and we loaded on boats at Southampton and went across on June 12."

He described the difficulty the soldiers had in getting through the 10-foot-high and 12-foot-wide hedgerows, filled with brier and brush, as they marched through Normandy, and at the same time, he said, the Germans would set up a field of crossfire from each corner of the area.

"But we made it through by virtue of the tanks," said the captain.

Waple also described the action he saw during the Battle of the Bulge.

Returning to the United States after the war in late 1945, Waple was assigned to the elite ceremonial detachment at Arlington National Cemetery in Virginia, and was involved in parades and honor guards in the Washington, D.C., area.

Then for a period of time, Waple was head usher for affairs of state under President Harry Truman, and was Truman's wreath bearer at the Tomb of the Unknown Soldier each Memorial Day.

"Here's a picture of Truman and his Panama hat and brown and white shoes," he showed the students.

In August 1948, Waple was assigned to the staff of Bradley, who by now was the chief of staff of the Army, and who later became the first chairman of the Joint Chiefs of Staff. On Jan. 12, 1952, Waple was commissioned as a second lieutenant by Bradley at the general's Pentagon office.

Waple was then assigned to the 3rd Battalion, 31st Infantry Regiment of the 7th Infantry Division in Korea, during the spring of 1952, and was in the war's last battle as the Chinese launched attacks on his battalion.

In late 1953, he was selected to be the aide de camp to Maj. Gen. Lionel C. McGarr, 7th Infantry Division. In February 1954, his position saw him serve as an escort for Marilyn Monroe when she paid a visit to the troops.

He presented the movie star with an army jacket, which Monroe took back to the United States. Waple said he was informed several years ago that the jacket he had presented to Monroe decades earlier was eventually sold in Chicago for $30,000.

He was promoted to his final rank of captain in 1956.

During 24 years of service to his country, Waple earned the Combat Infantry Badge with Star; the Bronze Star with two Oak Leaf Clusters; the Commendation Medal with four clusters; the Good Conduct Medal with 12 years of service; and several other service medals.

Waple concluded his presentation to the ROTC students with stories from his youth and a recounting of the experiences which led up to the time when he became a soldier at the age of 17 in 1938.

Waple has written an autobiographical book, *Country Boy Gone Soldiering.*

When I returned home, I told my wife about my talk and how well it was received. She suggested that I contact local organizations and schools nearby. I had early years, WWII, past WWII and Korea pictures that I would display at each talk. The word soon spread about my talks so I got calls from local schools, one of which had an ROTC program so I became not only a speaker, but also a helper in the program. I talked to the Colts Neck, Marlboro, Freehold, Shrewsbury and Monmouth Regional. The last school taped my talk that I just recently played for my wife. I, as well as she, thought it was great.

In June of 2002, my first wife, a veteran of WWII died. As a result of her service in the Army Nurse Corps, she was entitled to a full-honors ceremony in Arlington National Cemetery. With some help from me being an old timer in Third Infantry, we arranged for the Horse Drawn Casket, Full Honor Guard, pall bearers, firing party, bugler and chaplain. On this hot beautiful day, her ashes were placed in a crypt, a prayer was said by a Lt. Col. Chaplain and taps blown by a bugler off in the distance. Sad.

Even through there was a feeling of sorrow, it was a beautiful ceremony. I was proud to be there as at one time, those men participating would have been under my supervision when I was First Sergeant of the Ceremonial Detachment, which became "A" Company of the Old Guard.

I have a grandson, Dennis Buckley IV, who was a junior at Freehold High School in Freehold, New Jersey. During the second semester 2001, WWII studies came up. As the teacher informed the class about WWII, Dennis held his hand up and when recognized he told the teacher that his grandpaw was a veteran of WWII and knew all about the war in Europe. That and he was a hero and would probably come and speak to the class. After some phone calls from the teacher, Ellyn Lyons, a date was set. I went to work on my plan, a lesson plan, let's say. The program went over great, with Dennis sitting in the front row, grinning from ear to ear.

I also took two soldiers from Fort Monmouth in their full uniform of the day who answered any questions the students brought up. This was like a recruiting drive.

I followed this talk to the 2002 junior class and also with Dennis, now a senior, introducing me.

Another gratifying experience was when Colonel Hueler asked me in the absence of Major General Russ, Commanding General, Fort Monmouth, to present her son, Sam, the certificate for becoming an Eagle Scout. What an honor, it was for me in doing both. I had gotten to know the Colonel and Mrs. Hueler very well at the gold course, as well as Sam who during the summers played every day and became very good. He has been accepted to the Coast Guard Academy Fall 2003.

One day, I ran into a Captain Chew, the local district recruiting officer. Because of my attitude about the Army and "One a soldier always a soldier," he asked me to assist him in recruiting several prospects that were just on the edge of enlisting. I invited these young prospects to my home, told them of my life, the Army and great benefits during and following retirement. Of the three young men, two enlisted. Captain Chew though this was great. I then during my talks to senior of local high schools got many of the them to contact Captain Chew for details on enlisting. Chew reported my service to the Mid-Atlantic headquarters and recommend that I received a plaque from the commanding general of the Mid-Atlantic area at the annual AUSA meeting honoring all recruiters of this region. Again, I was proud "Pup."

**Receiving plaque from Commanding General N.J. M.G. Atlantic
Recruiting Commander.**

I was selected by the Retired Officers Association to accompany the Governor of New Jersey, Christine Whitman, along with about a dozen other WWII vets to Washington, DC, where the Governor presented Senator Dole a check in the amount of $580,000, a dollar for each New Jersey vet who served in WWII. It was a great trip, got to meet several other active Senators and other people of influence.

We drove down on a school bus and upon arrival, I noticed many sights that I had been familiar with over the years. I was stationed in Washington and drove General Bradley around town, especially the Capitol and the White House. Senator Dole, a veteran himself, noticed my Combat Infantryman badge with star and grasped my hand and congratulated me with a hug, stating it is always good to see an infantryman.

Another WWII veteran, Pete Rubino, accompanied me. After the check ceremony, we were taken on a tour of the Korean Memorial.

With children's cards from Waples Mill Elementary

I was diagnosed with colon cancer in July, 2002 and had an operation the first of October. I recovered from this operation in six weeks or so and then started chemo for eight months. Much to my surprise, I developed no side effects except as a result of the chemo, which performed weekly, made me feel "crappy." I could not taste my food, but kept eating to keep up my strength. I also did not stop working with my daily chores during spring, such as planting flowers and other yard work. If one has to be laid-up, the winter time is the time.

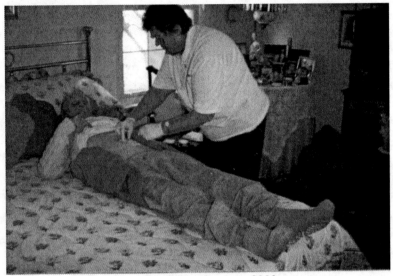

Recovery, January 2003

It seems that cancer likes me and my wife, especially her. She had a kidney out in 1995, a tumor in the brain removed in 1999 and an operation on her right lung in January 2004. All of this has kept ol' George jumping as I am not much on cleaning the house and playing nurse,but someone has to do it. I do what my best to what the man said, "For better or for worse."

When the Waples Mill Elementary School found out that I had a colon cancer operation, I received many get well cards. The sixth and the second graders have a Big Brother relationship and they all send me cards: get well, Thanksgiving, Christmas, and my birthday, on February 7.

The second graders ask all sorts of questions about my life at Waples Mill — how many and what kind of pets I had as a little boy and did I know any Indians? I could answer "Yes" to that one; my great-grandmother was an Indian and a beautiful woman. That was the winter I took chemo, so it was a great winter getting all of these cards, some of which I have posted on my office wall. I must have received well over a hundred cards, mostly handmade by the children. It was very assuring to receive a packet of cards just about every month.

Another great event of my life was when I obtained a letter from the Pastor of Vale Methodist Church, the one I attended Sunday School at and church with my mother. The letter asked me to be the "Home Coming Person" of this summer. Naturally, I accepted and on a bright sunny day in June, I arrived early to sort out the details and be given my assignment. I was to attend all three services, the first at eight-thirty, the next at nine-thirty and the following at eleven thirty. After the regular service, I was introduced and was received cordially. I thanked all for inviting me and gave a ten-minute talk on my past relationship with the church. I had the congregation crying and laughing at my quick tales of the past. Each service was told that I would present at the pot-luck luncheon following the services. I would say most returned or stayed for the rest of the story. I continued my tales of the great experiences I had relished at Vale Church. There were only a few people there that had childhood friends, but all were very interested in my story – what a great day, another chapter of my life.

Vale Church

In the late nineties I got a brainstorm that Waples Mill should have a historical marker, like one might see as they travel through the South.

I found out when the next Board of Supervisors would meet at Fairfax Courthouse and made a trip there. I stayed with a nephew, Bobby Waple, and he accompanied me to the meeting. After the meeting was about over and the chairman asked if there was any new business, I raised my hand. After introducing myself and before I could say anything else, one member of the Board asked me, "Are you George Henry Waple from Waples Mill? If so, I took your sister July to the senior prom." I knew I had a friend right then and there.

After much discussion, members stating that I was not important enough warrant a marker, who would pay for it, etc. I asked how much it would cost. The reply was at least fifteen hundred dollars but if approved the county would pay half. I told the Board I could scrape up $750.

The debate went on for several years with me corresponding with one member who was in charge of such projects. This gentleman, Mr. Hiller, worked hard on my behalf, finally selected the verbiage, location, and instillation of the marker.

Finally, after a dozen letters or so, we came to a complete ball of wax. We set a date. Now all of this took timing. I had to send invitations to all of the Waples and friends. I previously had met a wonderful woman, Mrs. Grace Karish, who had bought a new home on Waple land at Waples Mill. She and my niece, Odie Waple, helped with all preparations. However, the Community House had something else going on during the date we'd set for the unveiling. Another great woman, Mrs. Meyers, who had a new home in Papa's Old Garden spot volunteered to lend me her home, which was just across the road from the Marker for a small reception, though someone else would have to provide food and drinks. My friend Grace took the bull by the horns and put on a great show.

She sent invitations, gathered community ladies to bring different items. She and Terry Meyers, lady of the House, I am indebted to their wonderful gratitude.

Now it was Show Time, with a member of the Board, Gerald Connolly, Jack Hiller, my liaison, a hell'va man all in place, my family, friends, neighbors all in place, my son Gary said the invocation. Mr. Connolly said a few words followed by Jack Hiller. Then George Henry took over, what a proud moment it was to me. A boy who had been born and raised

George, Mr. Connolly and Hugh Waple unveil marker.

nearby seeing a marker unveiled at Waples Mill. During my short speech, I cried as well as my family. When the unveiling was finished and everyone shook my hand, congratulating me on the project, we went across the street to Terry's house for soda pop and cookies. It was great. I saw cousins that I had not seen in years. What a day. I have since put a photo of the Mill on a nearby board fence. If you are ever in Fairfax, ask anyone where Waples Mill Road is and visit the Community of Waples Mill and see the "Waple Mill" marker. "Yo'all come now."

In May 2005, I was selected by order of the Secretary of the Army, to become granted and assigned the distinction of Distinguished Member of the 3rd United States Infantry regiment (The Old Guard). He was presented the plaque at the Old Guard Reunion held at Fort Myer, Virginia just where he had started from. Colonel George S. Patton had pinned his Corporal Stripes on him in the same building in 1940.

I am not sure if anyone will understand this story as I've told it, as I am the only one alive today who has lived it. The only one with all of the knowledge of the research and experience of the times as I have lived them. So many little things that happened during the periods covered, that I failed to cover, but come to mind as I live on. I just wish that I could tell the complete story.

As I close my thoughts and memories I realize that I have covered a period of seventy years, 1926 my first Christmas that I remember, to 1996 the Christmas that I started to record these events of my life. All of these memories came to be as I remembered them. I have written for over two months and wrote my thoughts as they came to mind. I wrote most of these words as I normally speak them. I am to a point now where I sleep all night, not waking and remembering something I forgot. I'll have to admit that I have omitted certain events that happened during my life that I am not proud of and I guess maybe ashamed of. However, when I die and go to the place reserved for me, I do not believe that I will be last in line to enter the gates of heaven. God knows about my faults and also knows that I, in my opinion, am doing the best that I know how. Mama would say, "George Henry, you done good."

In the mid "90's my wife, Violet, suffered her first attack of Cancer in one kidney. After removing the one kidney and many months of recovery, Cancer struck again, this time in her head. Another operation and months of therapy she recovered with her beautiful black hair turning white, even more beautiful than her black hair was.

Several years later another pain, and Cancer was found in her lung, with another operation and more bad results. As the Surgeon's Assistant went down her throat as part of the operation, he severed one of her vocal cords and her voice box causing no speech and much more pain. She could not eat or talk for a long period of time without assistance. We had a special nurse, who specialized in eating lessons and talking, and with much rest she almost fully recovered.

In 2004 another pain came in the back of her head. After examination it was discovered that she had a tumor there. Two Cancer specialists and I discussed "what now"? They recommended another operation with the stipulation that she would probably have only six months to live. I stated "HELL NO, why should she suffer through another operation". They agreed. No therapy, go home, and prepare to die.

There was one thing she asked of me, that was for me to let her die at home. I had a regular nurse stop by three times a week and a nurse's aide four hours a day, seven days a week, leaving the remainder of time up to me. It was very difficult taking care of home, feeding her anything she could eat and taking care of her sanitary needs. As time went on she gradually got worse through Christmas and New Years and I requested Hospice help which was granted. Still coherent, she knew what Hospice meant, and one day, in February, when we were alone, she asked, "George, am I going to die?" With tears in my eyes, I went to her side, held her, and answered "yes". Holding her in my arms we both cried for awhile. When we could talk, I asked if she would like to see her children. At first she said "no", but after awhile she changed her mind.

I called her oldest daughter and asked if she would attempt to round up the other children and come visit their mother as she was going to pass on soon. Rene gathered up the oldest boy and the youngest daughter but could not get Ronald who refused to come and Peter, the fifth boy, was in jail. Andrew, the third child was a regular visitor. Rene called me back and I gave her a time and date for them to visit. The Nurse's Aide had their mother all prettied up as they came to the door. I led them into the bedroom and as they greeted their Mom all began to cry and I left the room. I could see that they were ready to leave in about a half hour; they all kissed their Mom and I escorted them to the front door. The rest of the day was emotionally very sad.

It was about this time that I asked for a hospital bed as Violet was becoming very restless, had difficulty sleeping and was in danger of falling out of bed. She balked at the bed at first, as she wanted to be near me. However, as she became more ill she became adjusted to the bed. Several nights later she got out of the hospital bed and before I could stop her she was on the floor. I did all I could to get her up and even though she had lost many pounds, I could not lift her. I called the Police who helped me get her back into bed.

As time went on she was sinking more and more daily to the point where I asked the Hospice Nurse to find her a good Hospice Home. This was done in late February; they were to come and get her, but due to a large snow storm the ambulance could not get to our home. That night I tried to sleep, but sleep was hard to come by as I was thinking that I had promised Violet that I would let her die at home. The first thing I did the next morning was to call Hospice and tell them to cancel the ambulance. To this day I believe this decision was one of the best decisions that I have ever made in my life. Violet was getting worse, and my night responsibility getting almost unbearable, but I kept remembering how much I loved her and would take care of her through thick or thin regardless of how bad the caretaking was getting.

On the second of March, at 7 O'clock am, Violet arose from her bed even though she was so weak, looking up at her mother's picture hanging on the wall and said "MA, MA,

MA". With this I jumped out of bed, went to her side, placed my hands under her head and laid her body back on the pillow. At this time she looked up at me and said" George

are you going to be alright?" With this, at 7:02am, March 2005, she died in my arms. I called Hospice, the Police, the Undertaker, which was one of my hardest chores in my life.

There was a Catholic service and burial in Arlington Cemetery several weeks later.

I received an invitation to speak at the Waples' Mill Elementary School at the Graduation Class located at Waples Mill, Virginia. On deciding that I could not drive, I arranged for a train trip to Washington On June 14, 2005, asking a friend to meet me at Union Station. Upon arriving at the

New Jersey train station in Edison, I got my ticket and proceeded to find a bench and started to read the sports page.

After finishing with the paper I looked to my left, greeting a lady who had arrived and sat on the bench. I spoke and received a cordial response from a lady who had a great smile, big brown eyes, and beautiful grayish hair. Our conversation started with small talk, i.e., where are you headed and why from the both of us. I told her that I also had authored a book telling of my life's memways. At this time I said, "my name is George Waple", she answered, "my name is Jeanne Florio". With the train approaching she asked where can I get a copy of your book? My reply was "right here"; $13.00 personalized and autographed". "ok" was her reply, and she passed me the money. I asked "how do you spell your first name". I received her reply "J E A N N E", so I wrote in the book "to Jeanne" just above my autograph".

As the train stopped she lead the way finding a seat for two. I asked her if she would like the window or aisle. "Window" she replied. However, as she sat we discovered the window was boarded up. She said "shucks, I wanted to look out". I replied, "that's fine with me as I want your undivided attention all the way to Washington"! I kept her laughing all the way to Washington with my life stories in addition to war stories. As we unloaded at Union Station I told her that I had a friend meeting me and asked if we could drop her off at her hotel. Hesitating, she finally said "ok", placing her luggage in the trunk I introduced her to my friend Ed Clark, a man who had served with me in the late 40"s. Arriving at the hotel, I got out and removed her luggage and escorted her to the hotel front desk, kissed her on the cheek and told her how nice it was to have met her. (We had exchanged phone numbers on the train.)

Since June 2005 we have become the best of friends, traveling to Florida where she has a home, to Nashville, Tennessee where I attended a book conference, to Las Vegas, Nevada where I attended another book conference, to Paducah, Kentucky where we attended a WW II Reunion, to Nashville, Indiana another WW II Reunion, and to Washington, DC several times to attend the Third Infantry Regiment, the "Old Guard" Association Reunions. While in Northern Virginia I showed Jeanne my old home at Waples' Mill, Waples' Mill Elementary School where I was headed when I first met her. We visited my great grandfather's home and my grandfather's home. We also visited my "swimming hole", Vale School, where I attended the first grade, the Cemetery behind Vale Church where we all attended Sunday School and Church as children, and the gravesites of many Waples.

And that's how I met Jeanne, my chauffer, my nurse, my secretary, and gopher.

Back in '62 when I was the Athletic Director at the Leavenworth Prison I was tackled by a prisoner during practice. I guess he wanted to get even with me for something. But anyhow, the knee bothered me and continually got worse over the years, so my

Orthopedic Surgeon finally convinced me that I should have a knee replacement. On December the 5th, 2006 I let the doctor perform the surgery. I realized how much the operation hurt in the Recovery Room. With Jeanne at my side every day I finally pulled through the recovery period in about three weeks and was home by Christmas. But let me tell you, if anyone says that knee surgery doesn't hurt, they are full of bologna! After returning home I still had to go for Rehab three times a week at a local Rehabilitation Hospital. Things did improve and I started to take Rehab at the Fort

Monmouth gymnasium on my own. Ten months later I feel like a kid with a new toy!

The only evidence that shows now is the scar across the top of my knee. I hope to be back playing golf soon.

Through my ambition to become more active in the late '90's I connected myself to Brookdale College, primarily to the History Department, Assistant Professor of History, Paul Zigo, and the WW II Studies and Conflict Resolution Committee. I am also now a member of the WW II Studies and Conflict Resolution Executive Council.

I have book signings twice a year in the College Book Store to help raise money for WWII Studies. I give lectures at the College, talk at all the local high schools and attend Professor Zigo's teachings of WW II Studies every Wednesday night if I can make it.

After all of these accomplishments Professor Zigo recommended me for an honorary degree to the College Board. It was approved, and on May 20, 2007 along with 1700 other graduates I received my degree. Another proud day in my life!

As the song goes: "I was born country and that's what I'll always be."

George in Cap and Gown at Graduation from Brookdale Community
College, Lincroft, New Jersey, May 20, 2007.

Brookdale Community College

Salutes all here present and by its authority awards to

George H. Waple III

the

Associate Degree in Letters

Honoris Causa

with all privileges appertaining thereto.

Given this 28th day of May, 2007,

at Lincroft, New Jersey.

George's Associates Degree in Letters

304

Earlier this year, 2007, I was invited to join a group to visit Normandy, France. Do to the fact that I had never been back since the liberation of the beaches, I thought I should go.

I was also encouraged, by a good friend to join her and her husband, John and Donna Coulson, for the trip. So on 9, July, 2007, we left New York City (Jeanne too) for Paris, France. We took a bus from Paris to Bayoux and checked into our hotel. I had a great trip, seeing all the beaches where the Allied Forces had stormed them on the 6th of June 1944. I was most interested in Omaha Beach were I walked ashore, June 12th, 1944. I was looking for my footprints in the sand, but I guess they had washed away! I did find a set of footprints that could have been mine, but I doubt it. The trip was a great success and I recommend it highly. The Normandy French folks were nice, especially to the four veterans on the trip. We visited all of the Cemeteries, Beaches, Memorials, Museums, and many other places of interest. I am very pleased that I finally got to see all of our landing areas and the history that goes with those landings. I do not see how we pushed the enemy off of those defensive bunkers and gun emplacements.

Jeanne and George at Omaha Beach

Four veterans at Utah Beach (George is second from the right)

George left his signature in a bar at Utah Beach

George presenting a copy of his book to a happy city official

George looking at his footsteps in the sand on Omaha Beach, where he
walked ashore on June 12, 1044. Or could they be?

At the close of the WW II Reunion 2006, 83rd Infantry Division, I was chosen to be first Vice President of the Association. I did not object as it was to be held at the Holiday Inn in Roslyn, Virginia on August 23rd, 24th, and 25th, 2007. The President and myself where in charge of the entire production.

Being Vice President, most of the chores fell in my lap, i.e., finding a guest speaker, for instance. With all of my contacts in and around Washington, I chose an old friend, a four star retired General, that I had known for years. He accepted but about two weeks before the reunion he became ill and could not perform. I then turned to another old friend, whom had just become Commanding General of Walter Reed Hospital, Major General Eric Schoomaker. He is also the brother of the former Chief of Staff, US Army, a four star General, Peter Schoomaker. At one time, at Fort Amador, in the Canal Zone, Panama, I was their scout leader. He accepted, which made me very happy. His talk was very informative as he brought us up to date on the conditions at Walter Reed. He also told us how quickly an injured soldier in Iraq can be evacuated to reach the medical help that he requires. This could depend on his injury as to how fast he received medical help, i.e., to a local field hospital, almost immediately, to Germany, for further medical help, in a matter of hours, and to the US in a day or so Jeanne and I arrived on Tuesday afternoon, the 22nd. We had planned to take a small group to Walter Reed General Hospital to visit with some of the Iraq wounded soldiers. I rounded up four individuals, at random, and Jeanne drove them to Walter Reed at 1200 hours on Wednesday. I'd made arrangements with a lady at Walter Reed what time to arrive, where to park, and where to go to meet her guide. The old veterans enjoyed their visit and returned to the hotel with some sad stories.

Thursday there were bus trips to Washington, DC that returned about 5 O'clock that afternoon.

On Friday we had permission to lay a wreath at the tomb of the Unknown Soldier. All of the old former veterans of the 83rd Infantry Division, their wives/companions, sons, daughters and some grandchildren were very happy.

With busses provided by the Third Infantry Regiment, we proceeded to the Ft Myer Officer's Club. After all were seated in the large ballroom, I had arranged for a quintet from the US Army Band (Peshing's Own) to play welcoming music. I then directed the Color Guard, from the Third Infantry Regiment (The Old Guard) in Colonial Dress, to their position. I asked the congregation to stand for the Presentation of the Colors. After the Colors were in position; I commanded "Present the Colors"! When they were in position, the audience faced the Colors and I lead them in the Pledge of Allegiance.

Followed by the National Anthem with music from the quintet, from the US Army Band (Pershing's Own). The guest speaker for the luncheon was Col. Joe Busche, the Commanding Officer of the Third Infantry Regiment (The Old Guard) at Ft Myer, Va.

His talk was not only interesting, but educational. He talked about the mission of the Third Infantry Regiment not only at Fort Myer, Virginia, but elsewhere globally.

On Saturday afternoon, after a traditional Mass, I had invited a Silent Drill Team of the Third Infantry Regiment, consisting of about 36 men, to perform for us in the large ballroom of the hotel. They were great! They put on a great show with flying rifles included. The 83rd spectators were thrilled! I received many compliments on the achievement for obtaining these men. After the exercise was over, they dropped out of formation and talked with the spectators, answering many questions.

The Saturday evening banquet went great! I had located a quartet who played professionally with dancing starting at 6:30pm to 10:30pm. By this time most of the old folks were ready for bed, as was I.

It was a great reunion, if I must say so myself!

Jeanne and I had breakfast with the Clark's, at McLean, Va. Ed Clark had walked the tomb for me back in 1948 (I was his First Sergeant). I fine soldier. I had three pancakes, two eggs, bacon, juice, and home grown tomatoes "HOOAH"!

It is now 10am on Sunday, my phone rings and upon answering it, "come out front, I have some veggies for you". I ran out to find an Old farmer friend, with a full head of grey hair as well as a beard, in fact, he looks like Santa Claus, bringing me tomatoes, peppers and such. Now, how often is this done any more? A good buddy, passing by, stops, gives me a big hug, saying, "how in the hell are you?, how is your knee operation, mine are killing me. Come by the farm anytime, Man, I miss ya, remember the old days when you'd drive for me?"

Before I close, I would be remiss if I did not mention a great friend and second cousin, John Martin, of Topeka, Kansas. He found me on the internet while scanning for the Waple family, from which he also came. Since we met through both the telephone and the internet, we have become good buddies. He praises my book as well as my upbringing, knowing from where I came and how my life started. I have learned, just from our conversations, he is a good man, well educated, and I believe, to have a few more "shekels" in his pocket than I. Yet, he is not one to brag about his good fortune.

311

His acquaintance has enlarged my outlook on life and how one should feel about life, especially, our kinfolks. So much, about John Martin, this story is supposed to be about me, not JM.

HOOAH!

Jon, Diane, Grant, Papa, Gary, and Carol.
My Family

Captain George Henry Waple III, A.U.S. Retired, as he looks at 83. He has rubbed elbows with many giants, one must read his book to appreciated his story. The sword behind him is the one he was carrying on the front page of the book. The white gloves are the ones he wore as number one pallbearer at General John Pershing's funeral.

Chief of staff of the United States Army greeting me in his office at
the Pentagon, September 10, 2004. We chatted for twenty minutes or
so about the past. I saw him go from a Cub Scout to the Chief of
Staff. We also renewed our friendship at the AUSA conference,
Washington, D.C. on October 25, 2004 as he spoke to all the
Sergeants Major of the U.S. Army.

George introducing Major General Eric Schoomaker, Commanding General of Walter Reed Hospital, brother of the Four Star General on the preceding page, who was a guest speaker at the 83rd Infantry Division Reunion on August 25, 2007.

George and his friend Jeanne between General and Mrs. Schoomaker at the 83rd Infantry Division Reunion Annual Banquet.

IN RECOGNITION OF OUTSTANDING CONTRIBUTIONS

TO REGIMENTAL CONTINUITY,

TRADITION AND ESPRIT DE CORPS

By Order of the Secretary of the Army

CPT (Ret.) George Waple

is granted and assigned the distinction of

Distinguished Member

of the
3D UNITED STATES INFANTRY
REGIMENT
"THE OLD GUARD"

PATRICK L. FETTERMAN
LTC, INFANTRY
Infantry Branch Chief

**Certificate of Distinguished Member of the 3D United States
Infantry Regiment "The Old Guard"**

317

Subj:	**United States Army National Museum**
Date:	12/7/2005 12:40:14 PM Eastern Standard Time
To:	waplegeo@aol.com

CPT (R) Waple:

My name is LTC(R) Jim Fisher and I work for the National Museum of the United States Army. I am in charge of the Veterans Programs and the Oral History Program for the National Museum (which has yet to be built). The new National Museum of the United States Army plans to open it's 300 million dollar facility in 2011.

We were intrigued with your book, "Country Boy Gone Soldiering" and might want to possibly use your story as part of an exhibit in the National Museum when it opens. We are particularly interested in your service during the period from World War II through the Korean War.

If possible and at your convenience, we would like to come to your home and film you and conduct your history. I will try and call you at your home in Eatontown, NJ (I once was stationed at Fort Monmouth and know Eatontown well.)

All the best!

Jim Fisher

Senior Strategist, Programs

National Museum of the United States Army

email from US Army National Museum

319

"Dance While You Can."

DEDICATION

The story of my life is dedicated to my lovely wife of 31 years, (Vi), who passed away on 2 March 2005. Vi was an inspiration and major support to me in creating this memoir. I do miss her so.

"Country Boy Gone Soldiering"

"Your story is fascinating. I simply can't imagine the level of responsibility you shouldered at such an early age – under very challenging conditions. It is evident that you endow 'Character' well beyond the rest of us mere mortals."

Lt. Colonel S. Wood, HQ US Army Garrison, Ft. Monmouth, NJ

"I enjoyed your book very much and intend to make it a 'Must Read' for my son and sons-in-law. They never had the pleasures of growing up in the 1930s and the early parts of your book will give them an understanding that I'm sure I have never conveyed to them."

Fritz Kroesen, Wife of Four Star General Frederick James Kroesen

"You certainly have had a rich and varied military career and have served your country with distinction."

Henry H. Shelton, Chairman of the Joint Chiefs of Staff

"You are also one terrific, delightful story-teller! All here who have had the opportunity to enjoy reading the book (and I have two in circulation, since Amazon.com finally came through), have declared it a winner. Its warm and humorous style carries the reader along the trail of your life with charm and flow, keeping us always engaged in the adventure of your career, and building admiration all the way through, from the spunky farm kid who was not put off by any adversity, but who made the most of all situations. You are such a nice person!"

Mrs. George Smith Patton

"Your experiences in many major military and peacetime events during your career are inspiring and educational. We will be very pleased to add this volume to our Library collection and make it available to cadets and instructors at West Point. I offer my congratulations on the publication of your book, and for the great contributions you made to the Army during your career."

Daniel W. Christman, Lt. General, US Army Superintendent

"I hasten to advise that we found your story not interesting, but fascinating; not moving, but inspiring - both candid and reflective."

Zane E. Finkelstein, Army War College Foundation Press

"This review was recommended for Army Magazine: "This is a book about high profile soldiering written by a soldier. As a senior enlisted soldier, George Waple held important positions within the leadership of the US Army following World War II. He offers insights into the lives of the giants that lead the Army at mid-century. Later commissioned by General Bradley, he went on to hold important positions to cap off a successful 24-year career. More importantly, this book is an example of the kind of communications we should encourage among our soldiers. It is a good read of a personal story. Obviously, the Army made him proud and in turn he made the Army proud. The autobiography of a proud and happy soldier cannot help but encourage future soldiers to join the Army. All of us soldiers can find parts of George's story that we can identify with - from combat ceremonies to retirement. I would like to see a hundred more personal stories like this on soldiering written by soldiers."

Neal Cosby, Institute for Defense Analyses, Alexandria, VA

"I have just read the book, *Country Boy Gone Soldiering.* I found it most enjoyable, personal, real-life and a picture of soldiering, not often portrayed and I think the US Army owes you a vote of thanks."

General Gordon R. Sullivan, (Retired)

"As I read your book, I saw in it and in you the best of those qualities for which this nation stands. For whatever it's worth to you, I am proud to have been gifted with the book— yet prouder still to have met its author."

Robert L. Nabors, Major General, U.S. Army Commanding

"This is a story well worth telling, the depiction of a lifetime of crafting rock-solid values and integrity."

Peter J. Schoomakcr, General, U.S. Army Commander in Chief

"Thanks so much!! You do indeed have a rich & fascinating tale to tell - What a career - What a life."

Colonel Gardiner, Commander, 3rd Infantry, Fort Myer, VA

"I would rather call you a damn good soldier!! I was impressed with your book. If I had known all that you had done, I would have called you SIR!!"

Major General George Akins, Retired, Ft. Worth, TX

"I spent last night reading *Country Boy Gone Soldiering* captivated by the experiences and pictures. Congratulations! Your loved ones are smiling down from heaven very pleased with you."

Ginger, Director, Mental Health Association of Monmouth County

"We enjoyed the pictures and the stories of Country Boy Gone Soldiering. The growing from bare feet to big Army shoes, who walked with 'Giants.' Congratulations."

Betty Guenthcr, Corresponding Secretary, Woman's Club of Colts Neck Inc.

"You and your book would be a wonderful feature story for us. Hopefully our paths will cross again."

C.C. Dyer, Publisher - Two River Times

"A Great Read."

Pat Buchanan - MSNBC and Former Presidential Candidate

"You have lived and are living quite a life – I especially appreciated the account of your experiences while working for General Omar Bradley."

Kenneth Cherry, Director, University Press of Kentucky

"I finished reading your book and I must say "you done good." First, let me say that you have lived an interesting life – Congratulations. It was fun to read your stories and to see all you have done. I am impressed. Also, I think you have a great outlook on life – I appreciate how you conduct yourself and how you treat others. I am also appreciative that you have taken the substantial effort to document and publish – I wish more people would do that. It is particularly interesting reading about someone you know. I am proud to know you.

Matt Balkovic, Retired, AT&T Friend

"Enclosed are letters from each of my classes expressing their thanks for your visit last week. It was so very kind of you to take the time to share some of your interesting life experiences with us. We are grateful to you for enriching our study of World War II. History came alive in our classroom. I wish you and your family a wonderful summer and I hope we can make arrangements for you to come and visit us next year for an assembly."

Lisa Wittman, Teacher, Marlboro Middle School

"The Writer shares a lifetime of a colorful family life, and his fascinating U.S. Army service which few soldiers have experienced. Highly recommended!"

Stan Bielen, WWII Comrade

"Thank you for all the information about your book. I was fascinated by your story, and have ordered the book.

Richard Howorth, Square Books, Oxford, MI

Thank you for the book. I have read it twice and was so pleased to learn so much about your fantastic life. What a legacy you have given Jonathan – I am so glad you took the time to write it all down. I am now sharing my copy with the rest of my family. Thank you so much again.

Love, Carol, Niece